Contemporary Approaches to
State Constitutional Revision

Contemporary Approaches to State Constitutional Revision

The 1969-70 Charles Hall Dillon Lectures
in Law and Government at the University of South Dakota

Lectures by
David Fellman, University of Wisconsin
John Bebout, Rutgers University
G. Theodore Mitau, Macalester College

with Transcriptions of Comments and Discussion Sessions

Edited by
Alan L. Clem

Report Number 58
Governmental Research Bureau
The University of South Dakota
1970

Library of Congress Catalog Card Number 78-631476

Published in cooperation with the Institute of Public Affairs, University of South Dakota. This publication is made possible by a grant to the Institute from Title I of the Higher Education Act of 1965 by the South Dakota Board of Regents.

Printed at Sioux Falls, South Dakota,
by Modern Press, Inc.

Foreword

A significant step toward the modernization of South Dakota state government took place on the University of South Dakota campus in Vermillion on November 14-15, 1969, when the South Dakota Constitutional Revision Commission held its first meeting.

The event coincided with the fifteenth annual Dillon Lectures in Law and Government, a series made possible by a generous bequest of Mrs. Frances Jolley Dillon of Vermillion in honor of her husband, Charles Hall Dillon, pioneer South Dakota lawyer, member of Congress, and Supreme Court judge.

The subject of the 1969 lectures, appropriate to the launching of the Commission's work, was "Approaches to State Constitutional Revision". The lecturers were three nationally known authorities on constitutional revision: John E. Bebout, former director of the Urban Studies Center and University Professor of Political Science at Rutgers University; David Fellman, Vilas Professor of Political Science at the University of Wisconsin; and G. Theodore Mitau, Chancellor of the Minnesota State College System. The lectures and the discussions were of such high caliber and proved so timely that it was decided to publish the proceedings in their entirety. Dr. Alan L. Clem, associate director of the Governmental Research Bureau, has ably undertaken the editing task.

A state constitution is an important factor in determining the quality of a state's government. South Dakota's Constitution is now more than eighty years old. Despite mounting evidence supporting comprehensive revision, two earlier attempts to call conventions were rejected by sizable margins. Most recent South Dakota governors, despite these earlier set-backs, would subscribe to the statement made by Governor Frank M. Byrne in 1913: "There is a very general feeling and belief that the time is fast approaching, if not now here, when there should be general revision of our state constitution, and that the requirements and limitations of our present constitution do not meet the demands of the people today for such governmental activities as they deem essential to their highest welfare."

The best evidence of the inadequacy and deficiencies of the present Constitution of South Dakota is to be found in the increasing number of legislative proposals for constitutional revision. In the November election of 1970, the South Dakota electorate will be called upon to vote on nine proposed constitutional amendments. All together over 150 constitutional amendments have been proposed by the South Dakota Legislature.

The establishment of the South Dakota Constitutional Revision Commission by the 1969 Legislature recognized the importance of constitutional revision to the progress of state government. The law directs the Commission "to provide for and enter into a comprehensive study of the Constitution of the State of South Dakota to determine ways and means to improve and simplify the Constitution."

If constitutional revision is to be successful in South Dakota, widespread understanding of state governmental problems is an indispensable prerequisite. The Dillon Lectures contained in this publication have already proved their value in guiding the deliberations of the Constitutional Revision Commission. They are presented here so that they may be available to civic groups and South Dakota citizens generally.

The Governmental Research Bureau is indebted to the State Constitutional Revision Committee for its cooperation in the holding of the Dillon Lectures and especially to Ronald Schmidt, Director of the Legislative Research Council, for his assistance in the scheduling of the lectures in connection with the meeting of the Constitutional Revision Commission. Professor Albert Sturm, then of the University of Nebraska and now at Virginia Polytechnic Institute, helped generate discussion of constitutional revision in South Dakota with his speech on "State Governmental Modernization and South Dakota" in the spring of 1968 (published by the Bureau in its quarterly *Public Affairs* series, No. 34, August, 1968). A large number of distinguished South Dakotans as well as South Dakota governmental officials participated in the lectures and discussion sessions.

All the participants whose words are printed here have had the opportunity to go over the entire manuscript, including the transcriptions, and their diligence in perfecting or clarifying language is greatly appreciated. We again thank the speakers for their generosity in allowing their lectures to be published in this form. Special acknowledgement is given to Mrs. Carol Kalinowski, secretary of the Governmental Research Bureau, for typing the manuscript; to Miss Mary Burns for transcribing the remarks from the discussion sessions; and to Miss Ruth Kromminga and Mr. Edward Toms for proofreading and other help.

It is our common hope that this publication will help the citizens of South Dakota strengthen their constitutional document, and further that it will be of use to citizens of other states in the ongoing effort to encourage government that is at once responsive and responsible.

W. O. Farber, Director
Governmental Research Bureau

Vermillion, S.D.
April 16, 1970

Contents

Foreword _____ v

I. Friday Evening: David Fellman _____ 1

    What Is a Good State Constitution? _____ 2

II. Saturday Morning: John Bebout _____ 15

    The Making of a Successful Constitutional Convention _____ 16

III. Saturday Morning: Panel Discussion _____ 36

IV. Saturday Afternoon: G. Theodore Mitau _____ 49

    Partial Constitutional Revision Through Piecemeal and
    Comprehensive Amendments: Reform Patterns of the 1960s ____ 49

Appendix A. Data on 50 State Constitutions _____ 63

Appendix B. Members of the South Dakota Constitutional
    Revision Commission _____ 65

Appendix C. A List of Participants _____ 66

The basis of our political system is the right of the people to make and to alter their constitutions of government.

George Washington,
Farewell Address,
September 17, 1796.

I. Friday Evening: David Fellman

DEAN HABBE: Our principal task this evening is to introduce the participants in our program, and I will proceed to that task directly. In presenting these gentlemen, one cannot help being struck by their competence and their truly national reputation in the field of state constitutional revision. One is compelled to ask, "Why our good fortune in attracting these three distinguished men to our state?" and especially compelled, I might add, in view of the early advance of the Dakota winter. One possible explanation, perhaps too pessimistic, is that the urgency for constitutional revision in South Dakota is so well known that our chronic case has attracted the attention of the top constitutional doctors in the nation. A more felicitous explanation, probably closer to the truth, is the general esteem in which the Dillon Lecture series is held, and more specifically, the ability of the Dillon Lecture committee to attract these distinguished experts to our campus. On this point I am happy to salute the committee chairman and, incidentally, my own department chairman, Dr. William O. Farber.

Our speakers tonight are especially qualified, because they combine the ivory tower approach with the grass roots approach. If I were to guess the principal reason why they are here tonight, I suspect it is because they have a genuine interest in promoting the cause of good government. They know, along with many others, that state government is in trouble, and that it needs help, and that constitutional revision offers one of the avenues whereby improvement can be attained.

The biographies of our speakers are set forth in the brochure which you have. It is not necessary for me to repeat their credentials. Our format is that the principal address tonight will be given by Professor David Fellman. Subsequently, I will introduce the other two guests who will have the floor for five minutes each. Tomorrow morning Professor John Bebout will be our principal speaker, and after noon, Chancellor Theodore Mitau, in each case with comments by the other two, and we hope, much discussion from the floor. We hope that many of you can attend all of these sessions.

And now our principal speaker tonight, a former Nebraskan, a famous teacher and, I might add, I have had the good fortune of having him for a teacher at the University of Wisconsin, a member of the governor's Commission on Constitutional Revision in Wisconsin, a prolific author and, indeed, a true scholar, Dr. David Fellman of the University of Wisconsin, who will speak on the subject: "What is a Good State Constitution?". Dr. Fellman.

1

What Is A Good State Constitution?

David Fellman
Vilas Professor of Political Science
University of Wisconsin

I

Ever since our national independence was declared and won, the American people have believed that government, which is not the state but only its agent, derives its just powers from the consent of the governed as set forth in a written constitution emanating from the people. Not only is the idea thoroughly familiar to us; the very words we use to express it are so completely standardized that it would be difficult to express it with any others. The Founding Fathers were familiar with written charters, the doctrine of the supremacy of the common law, and the concept of an even higher law of nature which is the ultimate measure of all things within the purview of government. They thought that government rests upon a contract, and that when its terms are breached it is rightful to revolt against government. All this was the prevailing party line in the period in which our basic governmental institutions took form. Thus in 1803, in the celebrated case of *Marbury* v. *Madison* (1 Cranch 137, 176), Chief Justice John Marshall flatly declared: "That the people have an original right to establish, for their future government, such principles as, in their opinion, shall most conduce to their own happiness, is the basis on which the whole American fabric has been erected."

On May 10, 1776, the Continental Congress decided to recommend to the people of the several colonies "to adopt such government as shall, in the opinion of the representatives of the people, best conduce to the happiness and safety of their constituents in particular, and America in general."[1] On May 15 the Continental Congress adopted a preamble for its May 10th resolution reciting that since it had become impossible to support any government under the British crown, it was necessary that all the powers of government should be exerted, "under the authority of the people of the colonies, for the preservation of internal peace, virtue, and good order, as well as for the defence of their lives, liberties, and properties . . ."[2] This is still a fairly adequate summary of what written constitutions are all about.

Like all constitutions, the original state constitutions contained a distillation of the political ideas which dominated the thinking of the Eighteenth Century. It is paradoxical fact, however, that while the Americans of the 1770's were involved in an overthrow of British authority, their first state constitutions were essentially conservative in tone, since they did not break much new ground beyond rejecting the principles of monarchy and hereditary aristocracy. On the whole, they sought to conserve the prevailing values of the age in which they lived. Furthermore, these first state constitutions were brief documents running from about five to about sixteen pages of ordinary print, and stating very concisely certain principles regarded as fundamental in a proper political society. These principles included the

---

1. *Journals of the Continental Congress*, W. C. Ford, (editor), Vol. IV, p. 342.
2. *Ibid.*, p. 358.

concepts of popular sovereignty; the separation of powers and its corollary, checks and balances; individual liberties; the supremacy of law; and among governmental institutions the concept of the superiority of the legislative body as the most authentic voice of the people.

In the years which followed, as old constitutions were revised, and fresh ones were written by the new states as they entered the Union, these documents changed to reflect mutations in the patterns of American life. Our state constitutions have always mirrored the various and changing conditions and values of American civic culture. One finds in them objective evidence of many important developments in American government, such as the growth in executive power; the erosion of popular confidence in the legislature, expressed through the spelling out of more and more constitutional limitations; the extension of popular participation in government; the rise of the corporation to a dominant position in the economy; the impact of the Civil War and of Reconstruction; the steady growth of industry and commerce; and more recently, the rise of great urban populations. As we move into the future our constitutions will increasingly reflect our mounting concern with such problems as race relations, water and air pollution, slaughter on the highways, the conservation of natural resources, and various welfare services.

We Americans are old hands at writing constitutions. We write them for social clubs, trade unions, church congregations, benevolent associations, professional organizations and even high school home-rooms. We wish to be protected by, and guided by, general principles which are spelled out in written rules of the game. In writing and rewriting constitutions the American states have had a great deal of experience. Louisiana is now living with its tenth constitution, Georgia with its eighth, South Carolina with its seventh, and Alabama with its sixth. Four states have had five constitutions each, and eight states have had four each. Eighteen states have had one each, but of course their constitutions have been amended many times. Only seven of our present state constitutions were drafted before 1850; seven were written between 1851 and 1865; the others were prepared after the Civil War, all but ten of them before 1900. Interest in state constitutional revision in our time has been stimulated by general constitutional revisions in New York in 1938, in Missouri and Georgia in 1945, in New Jersey in 1947, in Tennessee in 1953, and by the formulation of new constitutions since 1950 by Puerto Rico, Hawaii, and Alaska.

Our state constitutions, though by no means identical, conform roughly to a common pattern and employ stock words and phrases. The document invariably begins with a preamble which recites familiar first principles touching upon the nature and enduring purposes of government. At this point a reference to God is considered good form. It is interesting to note that God is invoked at the very beginning of our state constitutions and at the very end of every presidential inaugural address. Following the preamble is a bill of rights which spells out basic rights of conscience, of criminal justice, and of property in language which is thoroughly familiar to us through long and widespread usage. Generally, the next three articles deal with the legislative, executive, and judicial branches of the state government, usually in this order, spelling out their structure, powers and limitations. Most state constitutions have articles of varying length dealing with a variety of other subjects, notably education, the suffrage, public finance, and corporations and other business organizations. The penultimate article makes provision for constitutional amendment or revision. The final article usually contains a schedule for the transition from the old to the new dispensation. Since the Constitution of South Dakota involved the delicate business of separation from the other Dakota, its schedule (Article XXVI) was unusually long and detailed, consisting of twenty-three sections in all. Since it is reasonably certain that South Dakota will not be joined to North Dakota in the predictable future, its constitution could be shortened by nine pages through the very simple expedient of discarding Article XXVI.

II

That many state constitutions are seriously defective, and in need of extensive revision, is a proposition which finds almost universal acceptance among students of the American governmental scene. For example, a committee of distinguished scholars, after studying the New York Constitution, concluded that it was "literally amazed by the extent to which . . . [it] contains hollow phrases, defective provisions, and creakingly antiquated policies"; it concluded that 23 sections should be dropped altogether as superfluous, and that 18 should be rewritten and shortened "in order to achieve clarity, flexibility, and understandability".[3] At the same time the *New York Times* commented editorially that the state Constitution was characterized by "haphazard arrangement, slipshod and confusing phraseology, relics of long-gone fears, verbosity, frustrated efforts to fit law to new circumstances, a testimonial to the force of inertia".[4]

This is par for commentary on the over-all quality of most of our state constitutions. A very typical description of their inadequacies will be found in Professor Cape's succinct summary of the shortcomings of the South Dakota Constitution, which came to the following: "(1) excessive detail, (2) dispersion of common subject matter, (3) obscure and confusing terminology, (4) inconsistencies and contradictions, and (5) omissions and obsolete materials."[5] Similarly, speaking about the Louisiana Constitution, the most verbose of all, an able scholar has observed that any citizen seeking to study the document will run into many difficulties, including "the vast detail, the dispersion of subject matter, confusing terminology, inconsistencies, errors, references to other legal documents, informal amending procedures, duplication of material, contradictions and omissions".[6] Similarly, a California constitutional commission concluded, in 1930, that the state document was "an instrument bad in form, inconsistent in many

3. Inter-Law School Committee, *Report on the Problem of Simplification of the Constitution,* to the New York Special Legislative Committee on the Revision and Simplification of the Constitution, Staff Report No. 1, April, 1958, p. 330.
4. *New York Times,* June 2, 1958.
5. William H. Cape, *Constitutional Revision in South Dakota,* Vermillion: Governmental Research Bureau, 1957, p. 6.
6. Kimbrough Owen, "The Need for Constitutional Revision in Louisiana", *Louisiana Law Review* 1, November, 1947.

particulars, loaded with unnecessary detail, encumbered with provisions of no permanent value, and replete with matter which might more properly be contained in the statute law of the State."[7] In the light of such criticisms it is wholly understandable that when an Oregon committee on constitutional revision completed its survey in 1955 it recommended changes in all but 66 of the 232 sections of the state Constitution.

When the federal Commission on Intergovernmental Relations published its final report in 1955, it stressed "the fact that many State constitutions restrict the scope, effectiveness, and adaptability of state and local action. These self-imposed constitutional limitations make it difficult for many states to perform all of the services their citizens require, and consequently have frequently been the underlying cause of state and municipal pleas for federal assistance". The Commission concluded that there is "a very real and pressing need for the states to improve their constitutions."[8]

The Commission pointed up the central weakness of state constitutions when it observed that "it is significant that the Constitution prepared by the Founding Fathers, with its broad grants of authority and avoidance of legislative detail, has withstood the test of time far better than the constitutions later adopted by the states." The most obvious and the most serious shortcoming of most of our state constitutions is their excessive length and detail. They say far too much on too many subjects. While the original revolutionary state constitutions were short documents, ranging from 1,500 words (Virginia) to 12,000 words (Massachusetts), today 37 state constitutions have over 12,000 words each. The Louisiana Constitution, with about 236,000 words, is securely fixed in first place for verbosity, but there are other long ones, such as the Alabama Constitution with 80,000 words, the California and Oklahoma Constitutions with about 70,000 words each, and the Texas Constitution with 50,000 words. With about 25,000 words the South Dakota Constitution has the distinguished honor of being the thirteenth longest document among the states. In contrast, it is worth noting that the three most recent constitutions, those of Alaska (with 12,000 words), Hawaii (with 15,000 words), and Puerto Rico (with 9,000) are commendably brief, and thus reflect an understanding of what is most gravely defective in state constitutions.

Since the number of details which do not rise to the dignity of a place in a written constitution almost approaches infinity, a few examples must suffice. A very well-known case in point is the provision in the Constitution of South Dakota which authorizes a twine and cordage plant in the state penitentiary (Art. XI, Sec. 1). Another is a provision in the Constitution of South Carolina which defines what shall constitute a "durable hard surface" street in the city of Greenville (Art. X, sec. 14). The Oklahoma Constitution devotes 20 pages to the definition of county boundaries (Art. XVII, sec. 8), and 300 words to the piddling subject of free transportation by railroads (Art. IX, sec. 13). Many state constitutions spell out in precise sums the salaries of various public officials, as if the value of money never changes, and prescribe the popular election of an extra-

7. *Report of the California Constitutional Commission*, December 29, 1930, p. 9.
8. Commission on Intergovernmental Relations, *Report*, 1955, pp. 37-38.

ordinary range of officials, such as the Inspectors of Hides and Animals in Texas (Art. XVI, sec. 64). Many constitutions have excessive details on local government. About one-sixth of the lengthy California Constitution is devoted to city and county government (Art. XI), and the Louisiana Constitution devotes 28 pages to the government of New Orleans (Art. XIV, secs. 20-31.1). Public finance is another subject of lavish attention. For example, the Constitution of South Carolina describes certain debt limitations and then devotes 14 pages to spelling out exceptions (Art. VIII, sec. 7), and in addition has 12 pages of exceptions to the revenue provisions (Art. X, sec. 5). Many other subjects, such as highways, education, elections, corporations, and court procedures, are treated with excessive detail in many state constitutions.

All observers agree that the main reason for such verbosity has been the growth of popular distrust of the legislature. A great many of the detailed provisions in state constitutions are designed to prevent the legislature from doing things regarded as highly undesirable, e.g., enactment of special legislation, while other provisions are in effect directives to the legislature to do certain things they cannot wholly be trusted to do otherwise, e.g., the making of periodical reapportionments. To some extent, state constitutions have been lengthened over the years to overrule adverse court decisions, as in the field of labor relations and public welfare, or to forestall anticipated opposition of unfriendly judges. The expansion of provisions dealing with the suffrage and the popular election of more and more public officers was the product of the triumph of Jacksonian democracy. The rapid growth of public enterprise in recent decades accounts for the proliferation of constitutional provisions dealing with such matters as public works, the award of contracts, and the civil service. The steadily increasing complexity of the economy and social order has led to the adoption of provisions relating to corporations, public utilities, and social welfare. State constitutions have also been expanded to provide for the creation of new administrative agencies to cope with emerging problems of great magnitude. In addition, many constitutional provisions reflect the hopes and fears of interest groups who desire the security of special constitutional assurances. Occasionally an item is inserted into a constitution because the makers of the document want to put something regarded as especially important, such as homestead exemptions, beyond the possibility of legislative tinkering. In a broader sense, it may be observed that members of constitutional conventions often fall into the habit of assuming that in some special way they are endowed with more wisdom and righteousness than future generations are likely to have. Finally, it is to be noted that the American people, in the language of Lord Bryce, have "a conscious relish for power", and, as he observed, "there is an unmistakable wish in the minds of the people to act directly rather than through their representatives in legislation."[9] A democratic people seem to discover the means to have their way as quickly and surely as possible, even if that involves amending or rewriting the constitution.

It is the fate of a long constitution that in the very nature of things it must grow longer, for there is simply more to amend. A wordy constitu-

---

9. *The American Commonwealth,* rev. ed., 1913, Vol. I, p. 444.

tion must be changed frequently, which makes it wordier still. This explains why 460 amendments have been added to the Louisiana Constitution since 1921, and why the California Constitution has been amended 350 times since 1879.

It may be safely asserted that all informed students of American public law agree that state constitutional verbosity leads to many undesirable consequences. It tends to deprive the legislature of adequate control over its normal functions. It often results in needless administrative rigidity. The wordy state constitution is a constant invitation to litigation, thus adding to the burdens of the courts, and creating avoidable tensions between the judiciary and the political branches of the government. The more a constitution says, the more bases there are on which to challenge the legality of executive and legislative acts in the courts. Excessive constitutional detail also tends to solidify entrenched vested interests. It makes permanent matters which are actually temporary. It deprives government at all levels of desirable flexibility and reduces the sense of responsibility. It encourages the search for stratagems by which to circumvent constitutional provisions, as in the case of evasions of constitutional debt limitations, and thus tends to debase our sense of constitutional morality. It compels frequent recourse to the amending process, with all the expenditure of political energy that process usually requires. It hinders action in time of emergency. It often stands in the way of achievable progress. It blurs the distinction between constitutional and statutory law, to the detriment of both. It results in badly written documents full of obsolete, repetitious, misplaced, or misleading provisions. Above all, it confuses the public, and indeed offers the assurance that few will ever bother to read the document. It is asking much to expect the people to respect a document which they have never read, which they should not be expected to read, and indeed, which may be quite unreadable except for a tiny handfull of specialists. A constitution is supposed to serve as a great instrument for public education in first principles, but as Chief Justice John Marshall once observed, a constitution which partakes of "the prolixity of a legal code . . . could scarcely be embraced by the human mind. It would probably never be understood by the public."[10]

There are other flaws in contemporary state constitutions in addition to excessive detail. Many provisions have become wholly unnecessary and even obsolete. There is no longer any justification for provisions forbidding feudal land tenure, titles of nobility, outlawry and dueling. Nor is there much point in incorporating specific salaries for public officials in a constitution where another provision of the same constitution authorizes the legislature to change them and the legislature has actually done so.[11] Many state constitutional provisions have become obsolete merely because of the passage of time. A classic example is a provision in the South Dakota Constitution, which went into effect in 1889, which still directs the first session of the legislature to submit the question of woman suffrage to the voters. Many state constitutional provisions relating to transitory tax exemptions and state sinking funds are now archaic. Nor is there much point any longer in a provision relating to the disabilities of persons who participated

---

10. *McCulloch* v. *Maryland*, 4 Wheat. 316, 407, 1819.
11. Florida Constitution, Art. IV, sec. 29.

7

in the Civil War.[12] Some clauses are obsolete because the problems with which they were concerned no longer exist. A good example is a provision spelling out restraints on the construction of street railways.[13] Who in his right mind would want to build a street railway today? Another is the provision in the West Virginia Constitution that railroad officials are not eligible for membership in the legislature (Art. VI, sec. 13). This is the faint echo of a very dead controversy. A staff report of the California Joint Interim Committee on Constitutional Revision, 1947-1948, described 81 provisions of the state Constitution as obsolete, including a clause dealing with emergency relief administration in the 1930 depression (Art. XVI, sec. 10) and a clause describing the right to fish (Art. I, sec. 25).

All sorts of constitutional provisions are now unnecessary or undesirable for a wide variety of reasons. Some, such as a clause authorizing the governor to engage in war,[14] are invalid on federal grounds. Furthermore, it is wholly unnecessary for a state constitution to forbid slavery, since the matter is fully covered by the Thirteenth Amendment of the U.S. Constitution. Nor is there much point in declaring, as the Texas Constitution does (Art. III, sec. 42), that the legislature may pass laws to carry the document into effect. It is also unnecessary for a state constitution to declare that statutes which violate the constitution shall be declared invalid by the judiciary (Georgia Constitution, Art. I, sec. 4, para. 2). In addition, some clauses should be discarded or revised because they are wholly meaningless, such as the clause in the California Constitution (Art. V, sec. 6) which asserts that the governor "shall transact all executive business with the officers of government. . . ." Many state constitutions could be improved by correcting errors in grammar, spelling, and numbering, by resolving contradictions, by rearranging badly organized sections, and by eliminating the incorporation by reference of nonconstitutional documents. One need only contemplate the fact that two separate sections of the South Dakota Constitution are concerned with the pay of legislators, but that they are 36 pages and 18 articles apart (Art. III, sec. 6; Art. XXI, sec. 2). As for incorporation by reference, it has been estimated that the Louisiana Constitution gives constitutional status to 179 documents, including, for example, an 1889 statute dealing with sewerage in New Orleans which has been amended 10 times since its adoption.

III

It is incontestable that state constitutions, like most human contrivances, require frequent attention to keep them in tune with the times. Even state bills of rights are ripe for re-examination, for some deadwood can be eliminated, some gaps can be filled, and some provisions, such as those relating to the problem of privacy, badly need serious evaluation. It is essential that we give thought to other than traditional guaranties, to consider the need for clauses dealing with such matters as the right of collective bargaining, the right to social security, protection against various forms of discrimination, as well as against abuses by legislative investi-

---

12. West Virginia Constitution, Art. VII, sec. 20.
13. New York Constitution, Art. III, sec. 17.
14. New Hampshire Constitution, Part II, Art. 51.

gations. The ready availability of suitable remedies where rights are violated is another subject which ought to be reviewed.

Those clauses which deal with the legislature ought to be at the very center of any serious evaluation of the adequacy of our existing state constitutions. Above all, the very structure of the legislature requires attention. The issues here involve the question of the relative merits of bicameral and unicameral bodies, the problem of reapportionment, the improvement of committee procedures, and aids to legislation.

Constitutional articles dealing with the state executive are also in the area of active debate. What is basically at issue is the very existence of an adequate executive branch headed by a governor who can be held accountable for administering the laws. This involves a re-evaluation of the many boards and commissions sprawling all over the place, the adequacy of staff agencies and tools of management, the coordination of staff services, and auditing facilities. The dispersed character of the executive branch of government in most states is such that it can scarcely be said that an executive branch really exists except in some vague, mythical sense. Ancillary issues are also important, including those involving short ballot reform, longer terms of office, budgetary controls, the item veto, and administrative reorganization.

It is equally necessary to create a judicial department, something few states really have. What most states have, in fact, is a congeries of various types of courts with various sorts of jurisdiction. The main point made by the Model State Constitution is the need for a unified "general court of justice" consisting of a single supreme court department and other departments. Equally urgent is a review of the methods used to select judges, and of judicial rule-making.

State constitutional provisions relating to local government, and particularly the restrictions imposed on the legislature in connection with local government, need reconsideration. In this area what is needed is flexibility and decentralization, or home rule. Provisions are urgently needed to cope with problems of urban growth, such as annexation and consolidation of local units, problems of intergovernmental cooperation, city-county consolidation, debt limitations, local budgeting, slum clearance, housing, and urban renewal. Articles dealing with state finance should also be reviewed, particularly those which impose restrictions upon the legislative power. In addition, clauses dealing with education at all levels require attention, particularly insofar as problems of over-all administration are concerned. The efficient coordination of state educational services is one of the most important issues confronting the states today, and it generally is rooted in constitutional provisions.

Finally, the amending procedures set forth in state constitutions need attention. It is essential that constitutional change according to reasonable procedures be available, for where the amending process is too difficult to work the document tends to get out of date. On the other hand, it is necessary to avoid an amending process which is too easy to operate. In addition, it might be desirable to provide, as a few state constitutions already do, for automatic review periodically of the constitution as a whole. In connection with the whole subject of constitutional change, it is extremely important to provide for extensive research through the utilization of study commissions adequately supported by competent staff. Reliable knowledge is a condition precedent to intelligent decisions.

IV

It is no simple matter to prescribe the terms of a good constitution, and no state has ever had an ideal one. Certainly no constitution could possibly be ideal for all states, since all the states are not confronted with the same conditions and the same problems. Furthermore, a constitution must be both stable and flexible, which really means that it must not be so flexible as to lack desired stability, but not so stable as to close the door on adaptations as the need for change occurs. This is no easy assignment, to find a tolerable balance between stability and change, and in our kind of dynamic society there is always the danger that today's balance may become tomorrow's imbalance. This explains why the National Municipal League, which first published a Model State Constitution in in 1921, has found it essential to revise it periodically, so that by 1963 a sixth edition appeared.

I believe that the very first requisite for a good constitution is brevity. It is a great mistake for the authors of a state constitution to say too much, or to imagine that they are endowed with wisdom which later generations will never be able to achieve. A constitution is not a legal code, and it should not serve as a vehicle for the appeasement of temporary and partial interests. It should attempt no more than to state enduring first principles. It is sufficient that it describes in general terms the fundamental rights of man, the basic framework of government, and the procedures for peaceful change.

There is good reason to believe that contemporary conditions are favorable to achieve the goal of a concise constitution uncluttered with detail. Courts today rarely stand in the way of social legislation; there has been an observable decline in the legislative appetite for special legislation; the expanded reading of the Fourteenth Amendment of the federal Constitution sets nationally enforceable limits on many types of state misbehavior; and the modern mass media are tremendously effective checks on bad legislation and other forms of governmental impropriety. In all probability, a truly free press and political accountability through democratic elections are more effective checks than constitutional limitations.

Since one of the central purposes of a constitution is to educate the public in first principles, it follows that readability is a prime quality to be sought. If the average citizen is to be expected or encouraged to read the constitution, then it is essential that the document be written in clear, modern English, that obsolete terminology be avoided, that ambiguous phraseology be clarified, and that repetitious or contradictory language be corrected. The provisions of the constitution should be arranged in a logical, orderly, and sensible way. In short, a constitution should not be regarded as merely a lawyer's document, but rather as a people's charter which, to be read and supported, should be intelligible and even interesting to ordinary people. Thus it is wise to employ familiar language wherever possible, since the familiar engenders support.

A good constitution should reflect the best in current thinking about

10

government, and respond to emerging problems. A constitutional convention meeting in the 1970's simply cannot possibly ignore such matters as urban growth, metropolitan government, aids to legislation, court reorganization, reapportionment, ballot reform, the merit system, revenue sources, debt limitations, highway development, regional planning, conservation of natural resources, recreation, welfare services, mental care, and public housing. In all of these areas, change is in the air.

In addition, of course, the old problems do not go away. Bills of rights need clarification and modernization. Legislatures must be made more representative, and in many instances, smaller, and they should be organized along more efficient lines, and given more effective services. Relations between the governor and the legislature need attention. The executive and judicial departments should be made into true departments based on coherent principles of hierarchical authority. Much thinking must be devoted to the problems involved in the selection and tenure of judges. Intergovernmental cooperation at all levels must be facilitated and encouraged through institutional adaptations. Executive budgets, the governor's term of office, devices of direct legislation, and the age limit for voting are among the familiar subjects which need rethinking today.

Finally, it is desirable that writers of constitutions should stick as closely as possible to reality, and avoid the sort of rhetoric which stakes out claims and objectives which cannot possibly be achieved. Since a complete and uncompromising separation of powers, for example, is not possible and exists nowhere, it may be wise not to make such an impossible claim in the first place. Similarly, it is equally fatuous to assert that the constitution creates a government of laws and not of men. A constitution which makes such claims invites the prospect of becoming a mere snare and a delusion. As far as possible, a constitution ought to be a reasonable document. One may suppose that in the nature of things there is bound to be something of a credibility gap, because performance never quite measures up to the promise, but it is desirable to keep the credibility gap as small as possible by sticking closely to the realities of life in an imperfect world inhabited by imperfect people.

DEAN HABBE: Thank you, Professor Fellman. The first of our commentators this evening is Professor John Bebout, who has been long active in civic and academic affairs. Bill Farber tells me that he has been so prominent and so active in the National Municipal League Conventions that there is a feeling about that a convention wouldn't be legal without the presence of John Bebout. I believe that this past week he has been attending the National Conference in Philadelphia, and as you might suspect, he has been dealing with a subject on constitutional revision. Professor Bebout has been a practitioner *par excellence* in this area. He has participated in the workings of both the New York and the Alaskan Constitutional Conventions. In the one case I take it the efforts were a bit more successful than in the other, since one was adopted and the other was not. Perhaps we can learn from successes as well as from failures. At any rate, it is a great privilege for me to introduce our first commentator this evening, Professor John Bebout, formerly of Rutgers, and now from the

11

University of Texas at Arlington. Mr. Bebout.

PROF. BEBOUT: Well, it's a great honor and privilege to be here, but I really ought to sit down because it's impossible really to improve on Professor Fellman's very responsible statement on what's wrong with most state constitutions today, and what a good constitution, one appropriate to these times, would look like. Since he's been so responsible, maybe I can be just a bit irresponsible. I was involved in the rewriting of the National Municipal League's Model State Constitution the last time around, and I was involved in it a couple of times before that, or maybe more than that; I don't like to think how many times. And I had really become kind of tired of this exercise. So I said, "Look, let's write the right kind of state constitution." The right kind of state constitution could be written on one, or at the most, two pages. It seems to me that the first part of Professor Fellman's speech supported that view. As a matter of fact, my own personal opinion is that the best kind of state constitution would be one that wasn't written on *any* pages. In other words, it would be like the British Constitution, which of course is to be found in writings and customs and traditions, spread out through many documents, but cannot be found within the four corners of any single document. If it weren't for what may or may not be an unfortunate historical accident, we probably wouldn't have written constitutions in the United States today. However, we declared our independence and the new states had to establish a legal basis for their government, so the original thirteen, or several of them, drew up what they called constitutions which were really a writing down of the basic features of their colonial charters, or constitutions, or whatever you want to call them. Ever since then we have been revising these documents. And the more we revise them, the longer they get, the more detailed they get, and the worse they get on the whole.

Now, I suggest that the nearer you can come to going back to the first constitutions, as Dave Fellman has suggested, the better constitution you will have. It happens that my native state is New Jersey, I have lived most of my life in that state, and I am going to say modestly that I think it has the second best state constitution in the country. It is one of the shortest, it has less nonsense in it than most state constitutions, it deals mostly with the structure of government, it provides for a strong governor, a strong legislature, a real judicial department, and contains very, very few limitations on the powers of the state legislature. I think the best constitution is the Alaska constitution, which is one of the two newest, of course, and was in part an imitation of the New Jersey constitution. I want to suggest to you that these two constitutions, which are so fine and so similar, are constitutions of two states about as dissimilar as they could be. I suggest this because so many people insist that, "Well, my state is different and, of course, it can't use somebody else's—it's got to have a different kind of constitution." Well, New Jersey is the most urban state, it is one of the smallest states in area, it is one of the oldest states. Alaska is the second newest state, it is the largest in area and the least populous state, and they have the two most nearly similar constitutions. And they both, I might say, from personal acquaintance with both, are very happy with them. The last thing in the world they want to do in either one of them is

12

to change their constitution drastically. Well, I don't think South Dakota any more than any other state is going to imitate either of those two constitutions very closely because you're still going to feel, after all, "There's something about our tradition that makes it necessary for us to hang onto these fifty pages we have, or whatever the number of pages is, and these many elective officers, and so on." But you couldn't get a corporal's guard in New Jersey to support the proposition that we ought to have any more state officers elected state-wide than one; namely, the governor. We don't even have a lieutenant governor! And nobody moves away; the state thinks this is just wonderful.

Now just let me be a little bit more irresponsible. It has wondered me, as the Pennsylvania Dutch say, for a long time that the states which are supposed to be great experiment stations in government have never really experimented very venturesomely. For example, no state has tried to experiment with a very old system, namely the British Parliamentary system. And yet demonstrably it is one of the most successful systems or methods of organizing government in the world. Several of us were out in Hawaii a couple of summers ago as consultants to the constitutional convention there and we went around the island of Oahu one afternoon with a friend of ours who was a member of the convention. We were trying to dream up something that would make the Hawaiian constitution distinctive.

Well, we've had the one-man, one-vote rule, which in my judgment at least, makes the traditional American bicameral legislature rather pointless. Yet, I think there is something to be said for bicameral legislature, if the second house were like the House of Lords, even though the British seem at times bent on getting rid of it. So, we suggested something equivalent to the House of Lords for Hawaii, a Council of the Islands, since they have several islands of very different sizes, and it is important that each one of these islands has some sort of special voice in the councils of the state. However, under the one-man, one-vote rule, it's pretty hard to arrange this adequately in either house of the legislature, when both houses have real legislative power. So we suggested, as I say, an upper house, equivalent to the House of Lords, which would have debating, consultative, and advisory and recommendatory powers, but no real legislative powers. Well, our friend foolishly went back to the convention and suggested this to his colleagues. He reported two or three days ago in Philadelphia, at this meeting that was spoken of, on the reaction he got. What do you suppose it was? (Pause, laughter.) Well, I'm sure some people will laugh at some of the suggestions that may be made in this state. But I hope your Commission will be bold enough to come up with some ideas that it might suspect will be laughed at. And maybe one of them won't be laughed at, or if it is laughed at, it will be laughed at in a friendly way and maybe get by.

DEAN HABBE: Thank you, Professor Bebout. The final commentator this evening is Dr. Theodore Mitau, who is presently Chancellor of the Minnesota State College System. It is in this capacity that he is already well-known on this campus, for he was one of our speakers at the South Dakota Conference on Higher Education last spring. Dr. Mitau's publications are very extensive, including a very successful text on state and local government. He has been a member of the Minnesota Council on Constitutional Revision. It's a great privilege to have Chancellor Mitau with us. Dr. Mitau.

PROF. MITAU: Thank you very much for this generous introduction. The joy of the last speaker is that by the time he gets on there is really not much left to say. I felt that maybe we ought to summarize Dr. Fellman's exposition into ten short commandments regarding the make-up of a "good" state constitution. One: keep it short. Two: keep it flexible, but not too flexible. Three: keep to fundamentals. Four: keep it adaptable. Five: keep power fused or joined with responsibility; in other words, those who have power should be held accountable, and those who are held accountable should have power commensurate with their responsibilities. Six: keep it simple. Seven: keep it honest. Eight: keep your faith in your fellow man; not all of them are scoundrels, although a few might be, none, of course, in South Dakota. Nine: keep it in good, readable English. Ten: keep obsolescent material out of it.

And the attitude of your distinguished commission must be one of humility, a great deal of humility when you work with as important a document as the state's constitution. The evening is late and I have a lot more to say tomorrow afternoon. I will close with a quotation that I think all men in government should weigh very carefully. It is advanced by a famed theologian, Dr. Reinhold Niebuhr, who said: "Democracy is a process of finding proximate solutions to insoluble problems."

DEAN HABBE: Thank you, Dr. Mitau. That completes our program for this evening. I hope that all of you will be with us at nine o'clock tomorrow morning when the Dillon Lecture program for 1969-70 continues. Thank you and good evening.

II. Saturday Morning: John Bebout

PROF. FARBER: I'm very happy to greet so many this early. I hope we don't have too many administrators present. They might think that they could get this kind of a turn-out for regular Saturday morning classes.

A governor of Wisconsin was introduced somewhat facetiously as "Big Chief Cuttem Tax." He thought a moment, and when he rose, raising his hand in Indian fashion, he said, "How?". Well, this is often the key question. Last evening I thought Dave Fellman did an admirable job in telling us what a good constitution is like. But this leaves remaining the question of how you achieve that good constitution. While we will never be able to leave the question of what is a good state constitution, we are going to be concentrating this morning on this problem of "how".

Our speaker this morning is a man who has a unique relationship to the very first speaker in the Dillon Series. Sheldon Elliott of Yale University, in kicking off the Dillon Lecture Series in the 1955-56 academic year, talked of the role of the state legislature in the development of law. Elliott pointed out the unique importance of state legislators in the process of developing constitutions and law. But more than that, he pointed out how South Dakota had played a very important part in the development of the law-making process. Elliott recalled that David Dudley Field had developed his famous codes in New York about 1848. He couldn't get a "taker" in New York, but South Dakota became the first state to adopt, in the territorial period, comprehensive codes. I'm talking about the Civil Codes, the political code and the penal code, not the procedural code where some other states were before us. But Elliott in these lectures stressed the fact that South Dakotans had been innovators, that we have had a record of vigorous legislatures, and that looking towards the future we may anticipate that the legislature will continue to play an important role in the development of constitutions and law.

Well, both Sheldon Elliott and John Bebout, our speaker this morning, were consultants in the framing of the Alaska constitution. John has had a distinguished record of participation on a very practical level in constitution making. And so it is really great to have John here. I might say that the beginning of my long-time acquaintance with him was when we shared a flight on his way to Alaska. I was going over to Korea to tell them how to do it, and I soon found out I couldn't. He was on the way to Alaska to a more successful venture. It's a real privilege to have John Bebout here this morning to discuss the subject of staging a constitutional convention, and this will be followed by brief comments from our other two distinguished speakers. John.

15

The Making Of A Successful Constitutional Convention

John E. Bebout
Professor of Political Science
University of Texas at Arlington
(formerly of Rutgers, The State University)

In November, 1956, Emil J. Sady and I presented a paper before the Southern Political Science Association entitled, "Staging a State Constitutional Convention".[1] We felt some trepidation about using so "stagy" a title before an academic audience. However, some thirteen years and fifteen constitutional conventions later (sixteen if you count the Illinois convention elected in November of 1969), I am more than ever persuaded that we chose an appropriate title. Our paper drew heavily on the experience and inspiration we both derived from our service as consultants to the Alaska convention of 1955-56; and on earlier experiences, especially in New Jersey, Missouri and New York. I shall return to the dramatic analogy from time to time; in the meantime a few comments on the more prosaic title I have chosen for this occasion: "The Making of a Successful Constitutional Convention".

All the key words (making, successful, convention) require explanation. The "making" of a successful, or for that matter an unsuccessful, convention is a long, partly intended, partly unintended process, subject to traditional, legal, and political tendencies and constraints, some of which have roots deep in the past. It would be stretching things to try to trace the making of a particular constitutional convention back to the beginnings of our constitutional order, although I confess that my title was suggested by that of Professor A. B. White's great textbook, *The Making of the English Constitution*. A particular convention, is of course, but an episode in the constitutional history of a state. By the same token, it is an integral part of the whole of that history, shaped inevitably by the past, managed in the present, and hopefully oriented toward a viable and creative future. Much of the misunderstanding and mishandling of constitutional conventions can be attributed to a failure to recognize this truth. A convention may signal a new direction or tempo in the public life of the state and contribute to its form and substance; it does not create the basic forces or drives that determine the future. This was essentially true even of the most revolutionary of all American constitutional conventions, that which met to "form a more perfect union" of the states in Philadelphia in 1787. No state constitutional convention has approached that body in the significance of its own creative contribution to change; yet few state conventions have played utterly insignificant or purely negative roles.

This brings us to the meaning of the word "successful" in our title. What is a "successful" convention? The most obvious criterion is the submission of a revision or amendments that meet the customary test of success in politics, approval by the voters. By this criterion, ten of the fifteen

---

1. See an adapted version in W. Brooke Graves (ed.), *Major Problems in State Constitutional Revision,* Chicago: Public Administration Service, 1960.

conventions that have met since November of 1956 would be rated success-ful; three, New York, Maryland and the one unlimited convention in Rhode Island, unsuccessful; and two, Arkansas and New Mexico, undecided, be-cause the vote has not yet been held.

This is an impressive showing, but it leaves a good deal to be desired as a measure of success. On the one hand, it does not take account of the importance of the measures adopted or of their quality. On the other hand, it does not account for other possible effects, good or bad, of a convention whose proposals are not immediately adopted. And, of course, it does not tell us whether or not there might have been a better way to accomplish whatever constructive results were achieved. All of these ques-tions involve value judgments, as well as political judgments, which may or may not be the same things, about which reasonable people may differ. Constitutional conventions, like the piece-meal amendment process, have produced many changes in state constitutions on which the common verdict of history, for whatever that is worth, is favorable, some on which it is unfavorable. So far as I know, no one has ever attempted systematic comparative balance sheets for the two methods, and perhaps no one could. At any rate, for this occasion, this is the province of Chancellor Mitau.

Although I have not studied intensively all the adopted changes of the conventions since 1956, my impression is that in all or most of the states, they balance out on the "good" side. Others would disagree in certain cases. For many political scientists, the balance sheet for the pack-age constitution adopted in Michigan was a close one, and equally compe-tent students came down on opposite sides. I find myself with those who favored the new constitution, and my reasons illustrate some of the values of a convention that cannot be related to particular changes in the constitu-tion. In the first place, a constitution is not just a collection of separate legal statements. To coin a phrase, it is more than the sum of its parts. The New York Constitution was described in 1959 by a distinguished com-mission as "not a constitution in a proper constitutional sense", but rather "a mass of legal texts, some truly fundamental and appropriate in a consti-tution, others a maze of statutory detail and many obsolete or meaningless in present times."[2] Yet, that misshapen and greatly overstuffed document provides a legal basis for one of the most dynamic and effective state governments in the country. Something like this can be said for the new constitution of Michigan. The overall positive effect of the document was, in my judgment, to facilitate the toning up of a policy that had become victim of stalemate and loss of confidence. The new constitution gave the people and new leadership levers which they used to break old barriers and inhibitions to forward movement. If this sounds a bit romantic, I remind you that, on the other side, there have been those who in the name of realism have attributed the success of the Constitution of 1787 rather to the fact that it was launched on a wave of prosperity than to any quali-ties of the constitution itself.

Actually, the mere holding of a convention, if it is reasonably well planned and managed, can be a highly constructive experience for a state, even if all its recommendations are turned down by the people. Former

2. The Temporary Commission on the Revision and Simplification of the Constitution, *First Steps Toward a Modern Constitution,* December 31, 1959, p. 1.

Governor Jack Campbell of New Mexico told a group recently that he felt that the convention that just concluded in his state would prove to have been worth while even if its proposals are rejected at the polls. As I recall, he felt that the convention had highlighted basic issues of government and that its deliberations and the public information and discussions generated had already contributed significantly to civic education and enlightenment.

I have always held that the New York convention of 1915 was one of the most successful of all state constitutional conventions, even though all its proposals were rejected by the people at the ensuing election. That convention had the benefit of excellent background preparation, the leadership of some remarkable men and debate on fundamental issues of government not unworthy of the tradition of 1787. It served as a school for a number of younger men, most notably Alfred E. Smith, who later left broad marks on the history of the state. And as a not inconsiderable delayed bonus, many of the most important improvements that it proposed were later incorporated in the constitution via the amendment route under the leadership of Smith and others tutored by the convention. It seems altogether likely that a similar delayed bonus in piecemeal adoption of improvements honed in the convention process will accrue to the states of Maryland, New York, and Rhode Island, all of whose recent conventions saw their proposals overwhelmingly rejected.

Finally, let me add, we sometimes learn more of value in the long run from apparent failure than from quick glittering success. There is much study going on of the reasons for the recent "failures" in these states, and successes in others, some of which will be reflected later in this speech.[3] It may be that the setbacks in the three states just named will make a greater contribution to state constitutional development than the quick successes in some of the others. If the conventions in those states come to be seen in retrospect as having contributed significantly to education on the proper use of the convention and on the politics of constitutional development, they will certainly not be put down as unmitigated failures.

We now come to the last key word in our title, "convention". The sixteen conventions held since late 1956, or, in the case of Illinois, in the process of becoming, are a mixed bag. Eleven, including the Illinois convention, have been unlimited in the sense of being authorized to review and propose changes in any or all parts of the constitution. In New Hampshire, the convention is the only body authorized to submit amendments and the question of calling one must be submitted frequently (now every ten years). It is, therefore, atypical and tends, like the legislature, to deal with the constitution in terms of rather specific amendments. Five of the other conventions were limited by terms of their call to working over certain parts of the constitution. In New Jersey, the convention was called simply to deal with reapportionment in accordance with a mandate of the State Supreme Court. In Pennsylvania, the convention was limited to proposals on articles not previously revised by amendments proposed to the Legisla-

---

3. The National Municipal League is publishing a series of studies of recent and current conventions.

ture by the Constitutional Revision Commission. Thus, its function was to round out a well planned and phased general revision of the constitution. These conventions all operated under different constitutional and legislative enabling and constraining provisions, in different political contexts, with different levels of planning and preparation and under different ground rules of their own choosing. Obviously the relative "success" of these several conventions must be considered in the light of such varying purposes and conditions.

At whatever time the calling of a convention is contemplated, there are certain "givens", certain predetermined conditions that will go into the making of it. Other factors in its making will be in the future and subject more or less to planning and management, to civic and political determinations yet to be made.

Consider first the predetermined conditions. These differ from state to state, with differences in political climate; differences in the nature of the constitution, whether long or short, whether general or severely restrictive in dealing with structure and powers of state and local institutions; and especially with differences in the constitutional provisions directly affecting the calling, composition and conduct of a convention.

There is not time here to discuss at length the effect of political tradition which in turn is a function of the total cultural complex. The reality of this determinant, however, is a very good reason why an outsider, even an outsider from a state with many apparently similar characteristics, must be very careful about telling another state what to do and how to do it. I hope I will remember this as I proceed. On the other hand the people of any state should be cautious about assuming that, because they think it "different", their state should not or could not do something that another has done. The better I learn to know this vast country, the more impressed I am by the fact of state differences. But, paradoxically, I become at the same time more convinced that the states have hardly begun to learn the useful lessons they could from one another. What is good for one state may in fact be good for another of very different character, parochial doubting Thomases to the contrary notwithstanding. Let me illustrate. It would be hard to think of two states with greater differences in background and in governmental needs than New Jersey, one of the oldest, one of the smallest in area and one of the most densely populated states, and Alaska, one of the newest, the largest in area and the least populous of all the states. Yet, their constitutions resemble each other very closely, perhaps more closely than any other two. This is because the Alaskans admired the New Jersey constitution of 1947 and, without copying it, wrote their own along similar lines. Both states are happy with their constitutions, far happier than most other states.

How realistically the leaders of a movement for constitutional revision assess this factor of cultural background, including such elements as the level of popular participation in public affairs and the nature of the party system, and how they cope with it will have much to do with the making of the convention. The conditions may be given, but the understanding and handling of them will have much to do with their effect.

The same thing is true of the conditions set by the nature of the constitution to be revised. Correction of supposed deficiencies in the existing constitution is the central purpose of any convention. On the other hand, interests, real or imagined, vested in the existing constitution are the principal obstacles to corrective action. These interests pose the major tactical problems for advocates of revision. In general, the more detailed a constitution is, the more defenders of the status quo there will be and the more complicated will be the task of selecting a winning combination of high priority targets for change. This puts a premium on political statesmanship of a high order throughout the life of the revision effort. In some cases, as with reapportionment of the legislature in New Jersey in 1947 and elimination of a constitutional inhibition against a graduated income tax in Pennsylvania, it seemed necessary to revisionists to bar the convention from dealing with certain matters at all. Some people still dispute the propriety of these concessions to special interests, even though the prize might be vast improvement in other features of the constitution. Be that as it may, it should be observed that the provisions of some constitutions regarding the calling of a convention preclude, specifically or by implication, any such limitation on a convention. This is certainly true in New York and a number of other states. What the courts would say about this in South Dakota, I could not predict.

We now come to the constitutional prescriptions, if any, relative to the calling and conduct of a convention. Those in South Dakota are mercifully brief, leaving most details to the legislature and the convention itself. If two-thirds of the members of the legislature so direct, the people vote at the next legislative election on the call for a convention. If they vote "yes", the legislature is charged with responsibility for providing by law for the election of the convention, subject to the important proviso that the convention consist of as many members as the state House of Representatives, elected in the same manner, to meet three months after election. Sparse as these provisions are, they do set certain conditions that it may or may not be easy to live with. First, there is the two-thirds vote required in the legislature which in some states, has proved a difficult if not insuperable hurdle. Your constitutional timetable for action might or might not prove troublesome, if an urgent need for fairly fast action were felt. However, the fact that the South Dakota Legislature has annual sessions and presumably could provide for election of delegates at a special election means that the possible time span from the legislative vote to submit the questions to final action on the work of the convention is more flexible than in some states. The tying of the basis of representation to the composition of the lower house of the legislature assures substantial numerical representativeness but precludes experimentation with other representative arrangements, such as inclusion of representatives at large who have provided important leadership in conventions in New York, Pennsylvania and Missouri.

Now, given certain environmental, traditional, and legal constraints, what are some of the roles and options open to those who undertake to produce a constitutional convention? In beginning to explore this question, let us return to the analogy suggested by the alternative title of this paper, "Staging a Constitutional Convention."

A state constitutional convention, at least one with a license to draw on all or most of the constitution for its material, affords one of the more distinctive and expansive dramas, and a relatively rare one, in the political life of a state. Accordingly, it calls for a broad range of talents and tasks. Researchers, writers, directors, stage managers and stage hands, actors, a few stars, coaches and prompters, ushers, critics, a participating audience, a broader reading and reacting public—all will and should be there, in one guise or another. Perhaps in this age of mandatory television appearances, we should add costumers and hair stylists! As in the case of a play, the whole thing must be planned and programmed in advance; but unlike classical drama, although not so unlike some modern drama, the script remains fluid until the final curtain. And, as in the case of a play, the verdict of a diverse and unpredictable public comes later.

Now let us look briefly at the prerequisites of and the essential phases or elements in the staging of a successful convention.

First, there must be an idea. At the beginning, it may be just a vague notion in the minds of some people that the state could do with a better, more modern constitution. Or it may be a stronger, more precise belief that something should be done to eliminate constitutional roadblocks to desired action, or to correct flaws in the way in which official agencies mirror public policy. Sooner or later, the original idea or ideas must be imbued with a sense of urgency and focused on a goal or goals capable of mustering fairly broad support for a reappraisal of the constitution and an effort to improve it as an instrument for the time. In this, our time, the demand is for state and local governments ready and able to take vigorous action to meet urgent needs. This demand is currently re-enforced by the growing realization that in our system of partnership federalism we can not rely on national government alone for initiative, drive or even money. The Thirty-sixth American Assembly, at Arden House, November 2, 1969, observing that "most state constitutions need revision," suggested that "first attention should go to removing specific constitutional obstacles to state action." The Assembly followed this with a recommendation for allowing local governments to exercise all powers not reserved to or pre-empted by the state and for providing a constitutional base for vigorous and responsive legislative and executive departments.

Whether these and other desired objectives had best be sought through piecemeal amendment or general revision through a convention is a special question for each state. The answer should depend on the nature of the existing document and the provisions for changing it, as well as on the political climate.

At just what point the decision for a convention, rather than another method, should be made also depends on local circumstances. In recent years this determination has sometimes hung on the findings of a revision commission, much like the one now just starting its work in South Dakota. Often, it takes one or more years of study by such a body to clarify the issues, translate a general sense of need for constitutional improvement into concrete terms and point to the most feasible way of achieving the indicated objectives. A mixed commission appointed by the governor and legislative leaders performed this service in New Jersey in the early 1940's,

21

and set precedent that has been followed, with varying results, in a number of other states.

Ideas that can become a purpose and lead to a course of action are, of course, functions and tools of people. The "happening" of a successful convention, then, is caused by people, people performing as recognized leaders, many more people participating as involved citizens. The emergence and persistence of the right leaders and the readiness of numbers of people to become and remain actively concerned may make all the difference between an abortive effort and a highly successful convention. It took a combination of political leaders—three successive governors of both parties and others like Arthur T. Vanderbilt, later Chief Justice of New Jersey— and of literally thousands of concerned and organized citizens to bring about, between 1940 and 1947, the modernization of the New Jersey constitution. The organized effort of the citizens was coordinated by the New Jersey Committee for Constitutional Revision which came into being on a call issued in early 1941 by the League of Women Voters to a cross section of state-wide organizations. Determined leadership and wide citizen involvement are desirable, if not absolutely necessary throughout the whole process: the preliminary activities leading to the calling of and preparation for the convention, the selection of delegates and development of the agenda for revision, the deliberations of the convention, and the campaign on the adoption of the convention's proposals. For that matter, the process does not end there, because the implementation of significant constitutional changes through reorganization of the executive branch or of the courts or of state-local relations, as Governor Driscoll of New Jersey pointed out, may be an even more difficult and delicate job than rewriting the constitutional specifications.

It would be a mistake, however, to assume that the same combination of leaders and participants is necessary in every state. Indifference and even strong opposition in high places are to be expected and can be circumvented, provided the revision forces are able to seize the initiative and remain on the offensive rather than the defensive side of the issue. The overwhelming adoption of the New Jersey constitution of 1947, for example, may have seemed like consensus, but it was consensus won by determined and adroit leadership and civic battling, which achieved some victories by outlasting the opposition, some by strategic compromises at crucial points along the way. The more adept a convention is in imitating the men of 1787 in practice of the art of creative compromise, the more likely it will be to win support for a document attuned to a fairly high level of aspiration.

A crucial role in setting the stage for a convention is performed by the legislature when it enacts the enabling legislation. Within the limits, if any, laid down by the constitution, this statute will determine the composition of the convention; the time, method of election and pay of delegates; the time and resources available for preparatory and staff work, convention deliberations and presentation and explanation of proposals to the voters. In constitutional theory, a convention once in being may be master of its own agenda and proceedings; but as a practical matter, it would be very difficult for a convention to break out of time restraints set by the enabling act or to find money not appropriated by the legislature. And until the

22

convention is elected and assembled, its character is entirely determined by the acts of others.

An enabling act can be written either to facilitate or to impede effective performance. The recent convention in New Mexico was badly hog-tied by an enabling act that limited it to sixty days, the shortest period for any convention in recent history authorized to review and revise the whole constitution. It was further handicapped by inadequate funds for preparatory or staff work or for dissemination and explanation of the constitution. Informed observers believe that this act was deliberately written to make a successful outcome unlikely. Obviously, the friends of revision should do everything possible to secure an enabling act carefully designed for success. Precisely what this means in terms of election and compensation of delegates, provision for preparatory work, time-table and presentation of proposals must be thought out in terms of tradition, political circumstances and the nature of the revision hoped for. Observations on a number of these matters will appear in the following paragraphs.

It becomes a bit tiresome to keep saying that something depends on something else, but it is necessary in this business if we are to avoid the error of dogmatism or of generalizing from too few or inapplicable examples. So, in the matter of specific preparation for a convention, it depends in part on what has gone before. If, as in a number of states, the convention has been preceded by a revision commission that has made studies, held hearings and published recommendations, the preparation for the convention can be fairly limited. Whether or not a commission that decides to urge the calling of a convention should prepare a draft constitution of its own, is often a subject of debate in the commission. From the record in New Jersey, Maryland, Arkansas, and New Mexico, I conclude that a well considered draft by a commission can have real educational value, raise the level of future discussion, and give the convention a head start that can be particularly helpful if the convention is strictly limited in duration. Again, the amount of official preparation needed for a convention may depend on how much private work has been done in exploring and elucidating issues by academic and civic groups. However, there are certain highly desirable materials that in most cases will have to be prepared by an official body, taking several months in the process. The preparatory commission in Illinois is completing a thorough historical, interpretative, and comparative analysis of the constitution, section by section, that bids fair to become a model for other states. A somewhat similar document, prepared as a public service by a privately financed research group in Michigan, was an invaluable reference work for the recent convention in that state. In addition, a convention should be supplied with short objective discussions of major issue areas, roughly corresponding to the principal subjects covered by the constitution, with explanations of alternative ways of dealing with them. Finally, there should be a report on problems of organization and procedure in a convention, based on a study of other conventions, and a tentative draft of rules and of a manual on the logistics of convention management. Without such background work, a convention is in danger of wasting much time in the early days and of making snap decisions that may plague it for the duration.

Preparations of a more mundane order also must be made and may be almost equally important. The convention must have a place to meet with adequate working space for officers, individual members, committees, and the interested participating public. It must have supplies, equipment, recording and duplicating facilities, library, and maintenance and clerical and other staff. The convention should have as much command as possible over facilities and staff, once it becomes a corporate body; but the governor's office or some other appropriate body should be given the responsibility to make ready so that the convention can be effectively in business from the time it is called to order. The enabling act should anticipate these needs, which means that the proper roles of various agencies of the state, including the universities, should be considered in the preparation of it.

A number of states have demonstrated the value of preconvention briefing sessions for delegates on the unique character and problems of a constitutional convention. Illinois is about to provide such a session also for representatives of the news media, partly because the problems of a convention can be magnified by failure of the working press to recognize the differences between a convention and a session of the legislature.

In fact, differentiation between a constitutional convention and a state legislature is critical for the proper handling of a number of matters connected with the composition and conduct of a convention.

Consider first the selection of delegates. A common arrangement, sometimes specified in the constitution, as in South Dakota, is to put representation on the same basis as that in one of the houses. There is no point in discussing alternatives available in some other states, but two issues may have to be faced here if you consider a convention. One is the question of the role of the parties; the other is the question of the eligibility of legislators, judges, and other public officials. I do not think a simple rule can be laid down on either issues that is equally applicable in all states. However, the need to distinguish a convention from a state legislature, and certain other considerations as well, lead to two conclusions:

(1) party partisanship should be muted in some fashion, and
(2) legislators and other public officers with vested interests in the existing system should not dominate the proceedings.

Many states, even with highly competitive parties as in Illinois, have chosen to use so-called non-partisan elections in which candidates do not run, officially at least, as partisans. Others, like New Jersey and Pennsylvania have by law or inter-party agreement sought, with some success, to reduce partisan bickering by insuring a reasonable bi-partisan balance. This is mandated by the constitution itself in Missouri. It is quite possible that the story of the recent New York convention might have been different if Governor Rockefeller had not thought that his party would control the convention and therefore refused to enter a bi-partisan agreement something like the one that operated in New Jersey in 1947. When the Democrats unexpectedly won control of the convention, they were in no mood to do other than organize it on a partisan basis like a regular legislative session and to elect the Democratic Speaker of the Assembly as convention president.

A few experienced legislators, with a flair for statesmanship, can be very helpful to a convention, although one might observe that there are always a fair number of former legislators about. The same double-edged statement can be made about judges and other public officers. There can be no doubt that the large number of self-protective legislators and judges in the latest New York convention reduced the flexibility and, by their behavior, tarnished the image of that body. The same thing can be said about the presence of many legislators in the unlimited Rhode Island convention. In New York, the legislative members enjoyed double pay as a result of their dual jobs. The enabling act for the forthcoming Illinois convention does not exclude legislators; but it provides that no legislator/member can be paid a salary as a delegate. It is interesting to note that few legislators filed and only a handful will be in the convention. The Illinois Supreme Court has held that the governor and other top elected state officials may not serve and that judges must vacate their offices if they sit as delegates.

Each state must find its own answers to the questions raised in the above recital, but the questions should be answered in the light of the fact that, while a constitution is a *political* document in the highest sense of the word, it should not be a party document or a document to serve the immediate interests of particular persons. It should rather, provide a setting in which future party battles can be fought and future political issues faced under rules that are fair to all.

We are now ready for the first meeting of the convention. Hopefully, the delegates have had an opportunity to familiarize themselves with the background material that has been prepared for them and some of the likely leaders of the convention have done some careful thinking about rules and organization and conferred with the appropriate state officials about logistics.

By now, the time and place of the meeting have been set, probably by the constitution or by the enabling act. If the constitution leaves the matter open, it is to be hoped that the framers of the enabling act considered the possibility of a location other than the state capitol. The capitol may be the best place for it in a particular state, but the responsible people in New Jersey and Alaska are convinced that their choice of the state university helped to dramatize the special mission of the convention and protected it from the aura of "political business as usual" that pervades the capitol and its denizens.

Manuals on convention organization, procedure, and management and sample rules, can be obtained from other states or from the National Municipal League. I can simply highlight a number of vital matters observing that some of them relate to such humdrum details as seating arrangements, library space, visitors' accommodations, hearing rooms, and the like. As for seating of delegates, there is much to be said for the practice, recently followed in Maryland and Pennsylvania, of seating alphabetically, without regard either to party or to geography. It contributes to the desirable objective of developing in all members a paramount sense of identity with the convention as a whole rather than with particular groups in the convention. As for space, if the provisions made in advance are not satisfactory, the convention should not hesitate to begin its proceedings by demanding a better deal. It is the convention, from now on, that will be held responsible for its outcome. It should insist on the physical conditions and auxiliary services it needs.

Obviously, the officers should be chosen for the ability to lead, not drive, the convention to the highest achievement of which it is capable. The president, especially, may do much to make the style and spirit of the convention. Whatever his affiliation, he should command the general respect and confidence of the delegates and the public. In 1947, New Jersey found such a chairman in the president of the university. The latest Missouri convention, evenly divided between the two parties, found him in a highly respected lawyer rated as an anti-New Deal Democrat. Given that kind of president, it is wise for a convention to confide in him large discretion and responsibility in appointing committees, conducting the proceedings, mediating controversies and differences, and dealing with the public. The whole cast of officers, and the chairmen, co-chairmen, and members of committees should reflect the integral character of the convention. This may be done as in Maryland, by substantially ignoring partisanship, or in different conditions as in Pennsylvania, by a scrupulously fair sharing of leadership responsibility between recognized parties. The key word here is "sharing"; I did not say "division".

Experience of numerous conventions teaches a few simple but very vital lessons about standing committees. The first lesson is, the fewer the better. The New York convention of 1938 modeled its committee system after that of the legislature and came up with a host of proposals that looked more like statutes than proper constitutional provisions. If the object is, as it should be, a document as short and limited to basics as the tradition of the state permits, any convention should do well with from five to eight subject matter committees, a committee on style and drafting, a committee on rules, a committee on public information, and a housekeeping or administration committee—from nine to twelve in all. The subject matter committees should deal with large subjects in their entirety: legislature, executive, courts, state-local relations, rights and privileges, and citizen control. A convention with a very special problem in such an area as natural resources might, as in Alaska, find it desirable to set up a separate committee on that subject. However, experience shows that every committee will try to see its work enshrined in the constitution. Therefore, the more the committees, the longer and more detailed the proposals of the convention are likely to be, and the less well integrated into the so-called fundamental law.

All members should be on at least one subject matter commitee, and if the convention is operating under a tight time schedule, no member should be on more than one. In any case, two subject matter committees are enough for any member. Members may well be asked to express their preferences for committee assignments but preferences should not be allowed to unbalance committees either in size or in composition. It is a serious mistake to overload a committee with subject matter specialists. Lawyers should not dominate either the committee on the judiciary or that on style and drafting. Bankers and accountants should not dominate a committee on finance, or educators a committee on education, if a convention has seen fit to establish either of these perhaps unnecessary committees.

These and other observations are fortified by reflection on the special nature of a constitution as "the people's law", the law through which the people set the basic principles of organization and conduct for their government. Accordingly, the constitution should speak directly and clearly to and for the people in language reasonably comprehensible to the layman. The model is the Constitution of the United States, which necessarily contains a few words of legal art but which can still be read with more understanding and profit by school children than can most state constitutions that have been subject to repeated unimaginative legal tinkering.

Each subject matter committee and the committees on style and drafting and public information should have full-time professionally competent staff consultants and should have ready access to additional staff help from a pool of full-time and part-time people able to supply on short notice the various kinds of expertise required.

The subject matter committees should make provision for involving the public and for tapping the experience and ideas of especially qualified people in and out of government, including invited persons from other states. This means that the committees should solicit written statements and invite oral statements at hearings held early in the convention. Perhaps even more important, after a committee has developed some tentative draft proposals it should make them available to the interested public and invite written and oral reactions early enough to consider them before final convention action. This procedure in New Jersey in 1947 resulted in widespread feeling that the convention was, in truth, the people's convention, and it did affect both the substance and the acceptability of the constitution.

The committee on style and drafting has the very important task of harmonizing the style of the drafts from the other committees, fitting them into the constitution so that it has a logical structure, and pointing out any inconsistencies, conflicts, or duplications that might result from several committees working separately. It should start early so as to give uniform drafting guidance to all committees and to serve as a clearing house to alert two or more committees whose proposals might impinge on each other.

There is time for a few caveats on rules. Every member should be able to submit proposals, to offer his views to committees, and to express himself on any subject before the convention. On the other hand, if a convention is to come to a timely end, it must protect itself against time-wasting motions or debate. Hence, it was a mistake for the Rhode Island convention rules to stipulate that every delegate proposal must be reported on the floor of the convention. It is enough to submit such proposals to the appropriate committee, require the committee in its report to state its disposition of them, and provide procedure for forcing onto the floor any proposal that a reasonable number of members feel has not been dealt with adequately in committee.

Committee work and the tempo of debate and decisions will necessarily be affected by the timetable set for the convention by the enabling act or by itself. In turn, a viable timetable will depend on the nature of the constitution and extent of the revision contemplated, on the level of preparation and availability of professional staff, and on the spirit and capacity for self-discipline of the convention itself. Assuming the delegates are prepared to make the work of the convention their full-time occupation and assuming reasonably good preparation and staff, three months of actual work on location would seem to be the very minimum safe duration to contemplate, while five to seven months should be ample for general revision of a constitution of about average length or complexity. In any case, the convention will need to schedule its activities carefully, in phases, leaving room for revision of the schedule as time passes, if it is to come to the end with its task properly completed. These time periods are suggested with two qualifications. Whatever the time alloted, it will probably be desirable to stretch it out over a longer calendar span by providing for a mid-session recess of from two to four weeks, and also by extending the official life of the convention until the vote of the people on its work. The mid-session recess should be used to give the public an opportunity to study and react to tentative committee proposals and to enable delegates to take soundings of public sentiment. The Alaska convention used the Christmas holidays for this purpose. The period can also be put to good use for catching up on staff work, especially on style and drafting.

There are two reasons for keeping the convention alive after it has presumably completed and submitted its draft. One is to afford an opportunity to return in case some technical defect is discovered before the deadline for referral to the voters. The other is to provide a firm legal base for the continuing public information activities of the convention which will be discussed shortly.

One more thing should be said on the subject of time. There is important discipline in some reasonable curb on the duration of a convention, although the Missouri experience of 1944-45 illustrates the point that sometimes a convention may need a fairly long shakedown period before it can discover its identity and sense of mission. My own preference is for avoiding any absolute limit in the enabling act; but to set forth a tentative timetable which the convention may under certain conditions extend. Another approach has been taken by Illinois which puts no time limit on its forthcoming convention, but cuts off the pay of members after eight months.

How should the revision decided on by the convention be submitted to the voters: in a single package, in a series of amendments, or in a single complete document with one or more supplemental or alternative questions on separable issues on which voter judgment might cut across lines of opinion on the basic document? The last arrangement has been used to good advantage on occasion and was especially popular in the days when woman's suffrage and prohibition were among the most divisive state issues. There can be no doubt that if the revision proposed is extensive it is possible to produce a more symmetrical and more readable constitution by either the first or the third method than by a series of separate amendments. Symmetry and readability are qualities worth trying for, and the opportunity to achieve them may be a good reason for preferring a convention to the legislative piecemeal amendment method. The final decision on method of submission should be left to the convention and the convention should make its choice on the basis of the best political judgment it can muster. There is reason to believe that if certain quite distinct proposals of the recent New York and Maryland conventions had been submitted separately it would not have been so easy for the opposition to parlay a miscellany of discontents into a negative majority. In the New York case, it should be observed that the leaders of the convention erroneously believed that the very provisions which were largely responsible for the defeat of the document would actually produce a winning combination of minorities for it. This stands as a warning on the vulnerability of the political judgment of "practical" men.

As I have already observed, citizen involvement and public information should be vital and constant concerns of those responsible for promoting and preparing for a convention and of the convention itself. The convention's public information committee, acting under close guidance of the officers, should get into action fast. One immediate problem is to explain the distinctive nature of the convention mission and process to the middlemen of the media. Typically and understandably these people are prone to look at a convention through the jaded eyes and cynical lenses through which they tend to view a session of the legislature. Especially in the early days, long before the convention had found itself and come close to having tentative proposals worth reporting, the media are likely to muddy the waters by needling delegates for controversial statements that may be entirely irrelevant to anything that the convention may come up with. A sound public information program by the convention can do much to help the media do the kind of understanding and constructive job that most of them want to do. It goes without saying that the media should have convenient access to all meetings of the convention and to all hearings and official committee meetings. The committee on public information should not seek to make the news, but it can prepare releases and scripts and help the officers and members obtain timely access to radio, television, or the printed page.

This activity should continue until the popular vote on the convention's work. A convention delegate who has voted to submit a revision to the people has an obligation to explain actively and affirmatively why he believes adoption will be good for the state. The authors of *The Federalist Papers* set a good example that delegate-authors of state constitutions should emulate.

In addition to this more or less organized activity of delegates, the convention should plan carefully not only for the publication and wide distribution in pamphlet form of the revision or amendments to be voted on but for issuing a relatively brief official explanation of how and why the constitution will be altered if they are adopted. The conventions of Missouri, New Jersey, and Alaska have issued good examples of this type of document.

In a compact four-fold leaflet entitled "A Report to the People of Alaska from the Alaska Constitutional Convention," Alaskans were told not only about the chief features of the constitution but also about the essential purposes of a written constitution and the principles on which the convention based its work. Let me quote a few sentences from that Report:

In writing the Constitution for the State of Alaska, the Convention has determined that:

1. It should embody the best of America's 180 years of experience in self-government;
2. It should fit the special needs and traditions of Alaska;
3. It should be short and flexible, to allow for the great changes that the future will bring to Alaska;
4. It should provide for a government that is energetic in fostering

the growth and development of the whole State and the welfare of all the people;

5. It should respect and guard the equal rights and dignity of all citizens.

THE BASIC DESIGN

To accomplish these ends, the Convention prepared a simple plan of state government that is characteristically American.

This system in its essential features is very similar to that of the national government in Washington. This is because the Convention found that the state governments that worked best were those that conformed most closely to the simple design given to the government of the United States by the Convention that met in Philadelphia in 1787.

This statement of purpose was reflected with remarkable accuracy in the short, basic constitution, conceived in the classic tradition of American institution-building, under which Alaskans now live. They proved that, with some innovative adaptations, this tradition still has validity for a modern American state. It was easier for Alaska to go back to first principles in writing its first state constitution than for an older state to rewrite its somewhat battered document in similar terms. However, if the classic tradition is still good for the forty-ninth state, it might be equally serviceable in many of the earlier forty-eight.

PROF. FARBER: Very good, John, you've set the stage. I now present our next participant, Chancellor Mitau from our neighboring state of Minnesota, for a brief comment. Ted.

PROF. MITAU: Thank you, Bill. First of all, ladies and gentlemen, if you ever plan to have a convention, I suggest that you plan to invite John Bebout to be your chief consultant, because Professor Bebout is perhaps America's leading expert on the conduct of a constitutional convention. I think you could also have noted, and I'm sure you have as you listened to his observations, that this is a tremendous scope of undertaking, and if the state of South Dakota plans to have a constitutional convention, there has to be a great sense of urgency. As we used to say in the OPA days, is this trip really necessary? And I think that this ought to be under-scored—a sense of urgency, widely shared, widely acknowledged.

Now, what are the objectives? Are you wishing to strengthen the legislature? Strengthen the governorship? Do you want to innovate with new concepts of inter-governmental relations? Do you want to prepare yourself for the future of federal-state relationships which may be somewhat different than they have been in the past? For example, when I worked with the Governor's Commission on Executive Reorganization in Minnesota recently, we found that one of the very serious needs of the state was to ask the question, "What do we plan to do about the possibility of large federal funds coming to the state?" Should there be, for example, a joint executive-legislative commission on federal grants? One thing was quite clear, the legislature of my state was not going to give to the Governor the entire disposition of millions of dollars coming into the state. And in return, the governor very much wants a voice in what will happen to federal infusions, block grants, or other forms of federal aid.

30

There has to be very strong leadership; this is not a Sunday afternoon picnic; this is an undertaking that requires major political commitment. Your governor, your lieutenant governor, your majority leaders of the House and the Senate, will have to be committed to the idea that this is a necessary undertaking. I would say that there has to be a positive commitment of all the major political forces in your state. Your farm groups, your business communities, your political parties, your civic groups—they all have to believe that South Dakota needs a new constitution, and that change ought to be done *via* the method of the constitutional convention.

A few words about research. I think Dr. Bebout made reference to it, but I would like to re-emphasize the point. The research ought to be of a comparative nature. Why are the people of Alaska and New Jersey so happy with their constitutions? In a way we know the answer—these are constitutions that concentrated on fundamentals. They restricted themselves to providing for a strong executive, a strong legislature, and integrated court system and home rule—permitting the local governments to carry out certain inter-local relationships, and carry them out effectively. And then we should make a study of comparative failures. Let's see why some of these conventions failed when it came time to obtain voter approval of the results of their deliberations. There was the emphasis, and I think a very important emphasis, on the political climate. Whatever your deliberations finally yield, the climate will have to be one of the "bandwagon" effect—everyone is for this constitution, and everybody who is anyone in this state is committed to its ratification. People do not quickly discard their basic charter, under which they have lived for many years. With all its shortcomings, it constitutes a framework that gives a sense of satisfaction to a very significant segment of the community. I think we ought to make it quite clear that we are a conservative people. More-or-less all Americans are a conservative people. And before you start monkeying around with a basic charter, you'd better be very sure you really have a sense of commitment that you must make these fundamental changes. I would like to underscore further the absolute need for a small number of committees. By and large what is wrong with America's state constitutions in addition to their obsolescence, and length, and inflexibility, is the fact that we have too many provisions in them that spell out details that a short constitution would avoid. Five major committees should be able to do the job.

Perhaps one other point ought to be emphasized—popular participation. I think we are living in an era right now where people must have a feeling that they have a stake in the direction and substance of change. Political paranoia at a moment of great social crisis is certainly a universal characteristic. There are many very difficult problems before the American people and if a group of men are about to sit down for a period of three months and work on the basic charter and the people don't have a feeling that this is their constitutional convention, that all segments of the community have ready access to this constitutional convention, it would be very difficult to avoid the kind of back-lash, the kind of fear that characterizes so much of American political life these days. It's a very difficult question of whether this is a propitious time or an impropitious time. You can argue that a social crisis is a moment to avoid the discussion of as important a matter as the constitution. These are very difficult questions.

The bottle is half-full as far as the optimist is concerned, it is half-empty to the pessimist. In the final analysis, then, the whole thing reduces itself to what is feasible and practical. I would like this afternoon to go into the piecemeal approach as a possible alternative device that might work with a commission such as yours. You can, of course, go either way. What I suggest is primarily what may be called the piecemeal approach as contrasted with the comprehensive approach to constitutional change.

PROF. FARBER: We will now have comments by our speaker of last evening, Dave Fellman. Dave.

PROF. FELLMAN: Ladies and gentlemen, it is very difficult to come to grips with the substance of John Bebout's talk without moving into the area of this afternoon's talk by Ted Mitau. One of the worst things a participant in a symposium of this kind can do is to anticipate and invade the sphere reserved for the last speaker, who faces certain difficulties due to being the last speaker. A great many things will have been said by then.

I do want to say that I would be the last to take issue with John Bebout, either publicly or privately, on the subject on which he is probably the best informed man in the United States. I don't have that kind of courage, and indeed, there is nothing he said that I would differ with.

I would add a few thoughts, not to stir up a debate, John, but perhaps to amplify the picture of what a constitutional convention involves. I think that Ted Mitau has hinted at it, more than hinted at it, in his previous remarks. The thing that impresses me most, perhaps, about a state constitutional convention in a state that has been a state for a long time, is the tremendous amount of political energy which is necessary to carry that process through. I should add that I'm impressed by the fact that in any society, such as the society in South Dakota, there is only so much political energy to go around. You have to use it rather carefully. You may run out of political energy if you're not careful. It takes an awful lot of doing. Your first problem would be to convince yourselves that you need a convention. I would assume that if the commissioners on this new commission had a vote this afternoon, that it would probably be divided on this issue. Then you'd have to persuade two-thirds of the two houses of the legislature to agree to a convention. That's a most difficult vote to get, on that kind of an issue. Then the legislators would have to submit the question to the voters of whether or not they want to have a convention. If the voters say yes, the legislature then has to pass a bill to set up the convention, describe how the delegates shall be elected, how the convention shall be organized, paid, staffed, and so on. Then you've got the convention. And then you've got all the problems that Professor Bebout pointed out that are involved in redrafting your constitution. Then, you've got to sell it to the voters. You've got a tremendous selling job to do to persuade the voters that the new document is better than the old one. So, this involves an enormous expenditure of political energy.

I should add that I always worry about a convention because I don't think it can be assumed that the convention is necessarily going to be a superior body, let us say, to the sitting legislature. It may be better, it may be worse. I do know that there are many people who would never want to stand for election to the legislature, but who would be eager to

32

stand for election to a convention. There are some types, different types, that are drawn into that kind of one-shot work, as compared with the nitty-gritty business of grinding out legislation and budgets year after year, which is very hard work indeed. It is very difficult to anticipate what kind of people are going to get elected. I would never rush to any conclusions or make the assumption that you are necessarily going to get a body which is superior in civic quality, in intelligence, and in knowledge and commitment to the welfare of the state, than the sitting legislature. And I should add that improvement of the constitution is not necessarily inevitable.

There is a very good reason why university classes meet on Monday, Wednesday and Friday. If you meet every day, the soaking-in process doesn't take place. It takes time for ideas to filter through the mind and become part of one's intellectual baggage. But I think that the thirteen Commissioners, who are not under a time limit, can do a much better job of informing themselves than 75 members of a convention called with the proviso that it has to finish its work in 30 or 60 days. Your convention would have to be the same size as your lower house, which I understand has 75 members. So, since I believe that the generating point lies in minds of those who undertake the initiative in getting the process of constitutional revision going, I have much greater confidence that thirteen commissioners, taking their time and learning the business over a long period of time, are more likely to assimilate a body of knowledge about the problems of modern government than a one-shot Convention with a numerous body meeting for a short period of time.

As I read your statute (and I'm not here to interpret your statute for you), your charge is to find ways to improve and simplify the constitution of South Dakota. Section 5 says: The commission shall report its findings and recommendations in the form of proposed amendments to the constitution, to the legislature of the State of South Dakota, at its regular session, until, by act of the legislature, the commission is discharged. I read this to mean that your legislature in setting up the commission has, *sub silentio* at least, rejected the convention approach, and has asked you to study amendments and then to propose or bring these amendments to the attention of the legislature so that they may be dealt with in the manner in which you have always been accustomed to dealing with amendments. Now I don't think that any member of this commission would go to jail if you all decided, after you had worked for a couple of years, that it's hopeless to patch up your constitution, and that the best advice that you could give the state and the legislature is to forget about piecemeal amendments and go to the convention method. I think the commission could very well make that as its one and only recommendation. I can only say, in conclusion, though this anticipates this afternoon's discussion, that I profoundly hope that that is what you will not do, and that you will proceed with your charge to the study of these problems and study the document and to take your time to inform yourselves and then to propose amendments to the legislature as the statute suggests.

I would like to recount some of the experiences that I've had as a member of a similar commission, the Wisconsin Constitutional Revision Commission, in the past ten years. My experience is that this is a very hopeful way of going about it and is more likely to succeed than the other.

I want to say that I know that many states have had conventions and some have been quite successful; I would not dispute anything that Professor Bebout has said. There are some caveats that are involved in calling a convention, however, and I thought it might be worth a moment to call them to your attention.

PROF. GEARY: Professor Bebout, would you care to comment on the reasons for the failure of recent conventions in New York and Rhode Island to bring about constitutional revision in those states?

PROF. BEBOUT: As to New York, there wasn't any really well-thought-out purpose in calling the convention in the first place; in other words, they didn't have much of an idea. The legislature provided for bringing the call to the people because it was under the gun on the apportionment matter. Then, there were a series of mis-calculations. A friend of mine tried to get Governor Rockefeller to agree to take some of the political heat out of the election of the delegates by at least joining with the Democrats in the election of the delegates at large. We'd done this in both of our conventions in New Jersey in 1944 and in 1947. We didn't have delegates at large, but the leadership of the two parties got together and agreed that they would more or less divide up the convention the way the electorate was divided up. And they went out of their way, generally speaking, to compete with each other in presenting good slates of delegates. Rockefeller was so sure that the Republicans were going to carry the election that he didn't want this arrangement. Then when the Democrats carried the election, they weren't about to give the Republicans the time of day. The speaker of the Assembly, Tony Travia, a very ambitious man, insisted on being the president of the convention. If you read the letters to the *New York Times,* you discovered that some people voted against the constitution because they didn't like Tony, which doesn't seem to me to be a very good reason. But at any rate, he was an abrasive character in the convention, and to a great deal of the public. Then the convention was organized on strictly partisan lines, while the Pennsylvania convention, for example, was organized on a bi-partisan basis. It was treated more-or-less like a session of the legislature. Some very smart people made some terrible errors in political judgment. They thought that by submitting a proposal to repeal the so-called Blaine amendment, the provision of the constitution that forbids support to parochial schools, they would get the Catholic vote. Then they believed that by mandating the state take-over of the total cost of welfare, that they would get all the votes of the liberals and the people in New York City. And, you know, you couldn't possibly lose this way! Of course, a lot of Catholics voted against it precisely because of the repeal of the amendment, as many people told them they would, and upstate New York voted against the state take-over of welfare. So, instead of having a winning combination, they had a losing combination. Now, if they had submitted those two questions separately, if they thought they had to submit them at all, and maybe one or two others, it is entirely possible that the end result would have been quite the reverse on the body of the constitution. On top of all that, it was the most expensive constitutional convention in history, because the New York constitution improvidently provides that there shall be as many convention delegates as legislators and that the delegates shall be paid the same as the legislators.

There were some people feeding at the public trough, legislators, judges, and others, to the tune of $30,000 and more, by virtue of being in the convention. The judges behaved worst of all. They really put on a disgraceful show. They prevented the convention from doing anything really substantial on judicial reform. Between the judges and some of the legislators in the convention, they gave the enterprise a terrible image.

In the case of Rhode Island, they didn't pay the delegates anything, except a very small allowance for expenses. They didn't put any time limit on the convention. Rhode Island is a small state and you can get to Providence in an hour or so from any place in the state, so they just went on meeting year after year after year. And, in fact, I don't think that they have ever really formally adjourned. And they created a terrible image; so that's why I said both of those conventions were set up for disaster. It was planned that way, not exactly deliberately, but in effect.

PROF. FARBER: Thank you very much. We have arrived at the time for the coffee break, which will be served in the lounge. After we reassemble, President Weeks will take charge of the discussion session. When we reconvene, we'd like to have the constitutional officers sit in the front here, as well as the members of the Constitutional Revision Commission.

III. Saturday Morning: Panel Discussion

PRESIDENT WEEKS: Gentlemen, you will note by the program that this panel discussion does not call for a moderator, but rather someone to preside. And if there is no objection, there will be three rules that will govern this discussion. First, that your questions, your comments, or your criticisms should apply to the Constitution. That will give you plenty of lee-way. Second, that before you say anything, will you please give your name (and make sure that you give it loud enough) so that it can be recorded. Third, that no one, at any one time at least, give a speech more than three minutes in length. As far as I know, those are the only limitations that have been placed on this panel. We have here a number of members of the legislature, a number of constitutional officers, a number of lawyers, a number of members of the faculty, a number of students, and some other guests, so this is really an assemblage of potential comments and questions. And I don't know where these comments and questions can be dealt with better than by this resource group. We felt that we would like to have General Neil Van Sickle, who was elected yesterday by the Commission as temporary chairman, to take a little time (the three-minute rule does not apply to you, General) to tell us about yesterday's deliberations. General Van Sickle.

GENERAL VAN SICKLE: As I said yesterday, my principal qualification for this job is that I arrived at the committee room a couple of minutes late. But I can say that yesterday the commission met, got at least initially acquainted, and admitted to itself that its interests would have to be related to the timing of the legislative activity in the state, and that therefore it could hardly spend the time between now and April more profitably than by becoming acquainted with the problem.

We suspended our action yesterday hoping that we would learn some things from today's sessions and I think that we probably already have. So far, we have organized three tentative committees: first, one which will answer the question: "What must we do to insure that the public and we, ourselves, understand what we are trying to do?" The second one answers the question: "What ought the scope of research to be?" And a third committee will answer the question: "What do we need and how are we going to pay for it?" I think it is appropriate to say right now that we see in the University of South Dakota an opportunity to tap graduate students' energies and ideas very substantially in this work. That opportunity is one of our great advantages. Thank you.

PRESIDENT WEEKS: Now, the panel is open. I see Bernard Linn, who for I don't know how long has been South Dakota's Commissioner of School and Public Lands. He made the statement publicly some time ago that he was not going to be a candidate again, so I assume that he is in a pretty good position to say what he would like to say about the Constitution of the State of South Dakota. Commissioner Linn.

MR. LINN: President Weeks, distinguished visitors. When Dr. Farber sent me a letter inviting me to this meeting, he wrote down at the bottom, "I think you should be here." I think enough of Dr. Farber that I do pretty much what he thinks I ought to do.

I came down here anticipating that I would learn a great deal that I didn't know about the constitution, and that was an understatement. I feel already, without the lectures this afternoon, somewhat like a mosquito that asked for a drink of water and got it with a fire hose. I have been attempting to assimilate everything that has been said and think that within a year or two I will know pretty well, and get the significance of, what has been said. With a little bit of fear and trembling I have listened for quotations, fearing, as so often happens, that a quotation that I wanted to make would be made by someone else. Now, I may surprise some of you people in two ways. First, I'm going to quote from a Democrat. And second, I think that it gives us a "go ahead" on what we are trying to do. I am quoting Thomas Jefferson: "Some men look at constitutions with sanctimonious reverence, and deem them like the ark of the Covenant, too sacred to be touched. They ascribe to the men of the preceeding age a wisdom more than human, and suppose what they did to be beyond amendment. Laws and institutions must go hand-in-hand with the progress of the human mind. We might as well require a man to wear the coat that fitted him as a boy as ask civilized society to remain ever under the regime of their ancestors." So he told us to amend our constitutions! Keep them up with current conditions.

It is often said that we have an eighty-year-old constitution. Well, of course, that isn't so. Last fall we passed Amendment D so that part of the constitution is less than one year old. And as you have been told, it has been amended 75 times.

My only admonition to the Commission is something that is not necessary. I know that they are very, very conscious of it. In the body of the constitution be careful of what you do. In the preamble to the constitution be especially careful of what you do. In the Bill of Rights be even more careful of what you do. And be sure that if and when the constitution is amended in the next two or three or five or seven years that the motto of the state of South Dakota can still be "Under God the People Rule".

PRESIDENT WEEKS: Thank you, Bernard. There must be some questions or comments that you want to direct to some of these resource people. Mr. Lacey.

REPRESENTATIVE LACEY: May I begin with a basic question? I think we can all benefit from a discussion of how best can we begin this task.

PROF. BEBOUT: It seems to me that you have indicated that you're making what I would regard as the correct start, which is to familiarize yourselves as individuals with the constitution as a whole and in all its parts. It seems to me that you'd need to get an over-view of it before you can begin to pick out the particular targets that you want to concentrate on, and you want also to be sure that whatever you do to one part, you take into account its effect on other parts. All constitutions are to some extent interlocking, and the reason that they are interlocking on a given subject may be principally because the subject is also dealt with, explicitly may have repercussions on other articles. But first I think you need to or implicitly, in several articles. What you do to the article on the executive may have repercussions on other articles. But first I think you need to understand the effect of the constitution as a whole.

PRESIDENT WEEKS: Yes, Dr. Fellman.

PROF. FELLMAN: One of the peculiarities about your constitution is that an awful lot of it is obsolete, an unusually large portion of it. You probably have more obsolete stuff in your constitution than any other constitution of comparable length. And, the thought occurred to me that you might have a committee on style, merely for the purpose of cleaning up and tidying up the document. As I read your constitution here, the problem was that you were part of the territory of Dakota, then you were split in half. Many of the provisions, not only in the schedule which I mentioned last night, but in the body of the constitution also, relate to the painful process you had of separating North Dakota from South Dakota. Assuming that the separation of North Dakota and South Dakota is here to stay, (I have detected no movement to make one state out of the two), there is a lot of obsolete stuff that can be pulled out, and that would be the easiest job in my opinion. I think a committee on style that worked through the whole document merely in terms of style would be a very useful thing to have.

PROFESSOR BEBOUT: I'd like to comment on that a little further. I was director of the Temporary Commission on Revision and Simplification of the Constitution of New York. That's a hell of a long title for a commission devoted to simplification. This operated for about four years— from 1957 to 1961. Now a few of the amendments proposed by way of simplification and the deletion of obsolete material have been adopted. But in this case we recognized that with respect to the New York constitution the problem of simplification was a very complicated one and that people might differ about what is obsolete and what is not obsolete. So we managed to trap deans of the principal law schools in the state into putting the finger on some top law professors, who became an *ad hoc* group on the problem of simplification. I suggest that you ought to get hold of that document, "The Inter-Law School Committee Report on the Simplification of the Constitution of New York". I'm not sure where you can get it, but if you can't get it from the state, I'm sure that the National Municipal League at 47 East 68th Street in New York City has a few copies and it could at least spare one or two. If you can't get it from them, I have some in the cellar of my former office in New Brunswick and I could probably induce my former secretary to dig them out. Now as I say, some things that you think are obsolete may not appear to be obsolete to others. For example, we wanted to get the canal article out of the constitution of New York, and we finally did, I guess, but we had a terrible time persuading the lovers of the canal that this wasn't sacred stuff. We thought it was foolish to continue in the constitution a provision on workmen's compensation which has long since been in effect superseded, because legislation had gone way beyond the constitutional provision on workmen's compensation. The

Labor Unions served notice, that if we touched a word in that sacred provision they'd go out and beat everything we wanted to do and we just drew back. Well, o.k. It's a tough cause.

JUDGE FOSHEIM: Is a Bill of Rights in a state constitution necessary in those areas where the Bill of Rights of the U. S. Constitution has been held applicable to and binding upon the states under the 14th Amendment?

PROF. FELLMAN: Every state constitution has a Bill of Rights which is more or less the same as the federal model. Now, for the last few years our Supreme Court has made a series of decisions, which have incorporated practically all, but not all, of the provisions of the federal Bill of Rights into the Due Process clause of the 14th Amendment, thus making them enforceable limitations upon the states.

What is the point then, of adding a duplicate and separate Bill of Rights to the state constitution if the federal Bill of Rights is binding on the states anyway? The drift of Supreme Court decisions is not all that clear. For example, the Supreme Court just held this past term, for the first time that the right to trial by jury is a due-process right, and that a state may not deny it in the case of any serious offense. A lot of questions are left wide open, however, which are still under state law. For example, the Supreme Court did not say that every aspect of jury trial, as understood in federal jurisprudence, now applies to the states. The right of jury trial does now apply in serious offenses, but the Court didn't say where it would draw the line between serious and petty offenses. Presumably, in future litigation, it may work that out. In any event, regarding petty offenses, the whole matter is left to the state. A jury trial in the federal court, as the Supreme Court has always said, requires a jury of twelve. Now, many states have juries with less than twelve. Under some circumstances, in my state, we may have juries of six; Utah has juries of eight; and some have juries of ten. Furthermore, in a jury trial in a federal court, conviction requires the unanimous vote of the jury. But a number of states permit decisions of the jury by a less than unanimous vote, even in criminal cases. We have at least five states that permit conviction in criminal cases by less than a unanimous vote of the jury. Many states have provisions for verdicts in civil cases by less than a unanimous vote. I think you have such verdicts in South Dakota, don't you? In Wisconsin a civil jury may give judgment by a vote of ten. And another state that I know of requires that a jury be unanimous in a civil case for the first four hours, but after the jury has been out for four hours it may reach a decision by a vote of ten. Well, there are a great many variations in the jury system. So it is not all that clear that the *Duncan* decision of the U. S. Supreme Court settles the matter. The states don't have to be concerned that all the rules are going to be made by the United States Supreme Court. I should think that even where you have incorporation, and the process has gone a long distance, that that doesn't mean that the body of due process law which the U. S. Supreme Court has read into the 14th Amendment makes the state bills of rights and state statutory codes unnecessary or out-of-date. I don't think the process has gone that far, or will ever go that far.

PRESIDENT WEEKS: Someone else? We have representatives here of all

39

three branches of the state government, so there must be some comments that someone wishes to make. Yes? Dr. Clem.

PROFESSOR CLEM: I don't know to whom I should address this question—legislators, panelists, commission members, faculty members or students. There has been some talk from all of the panelists to the effect that all states believe that they have some particular, unique, local kind of problem which they feel the state constitutional document must give special attention to. For example, it has been mentioned that in Alaska a need was felt for special attention to natural resources in the constitutional document. Perhaps it is not quite appropriate to ask a visiting panelist from New Jersey, Wisconsin, or Minnesota what it is about South Dakota that most requires special consideration and treatment. I wonder if any of you here, especially members of the commission, would want to comment on what you think it is about South Dakota that might require special attention in constitutional revision?

PRESIDENT WEEKS: Is there anyone who would care to respond to that? Perhaps some of the constitutional officers might like to respond to that, if not members of the committee. Mr. Linn.

MR. LINN: It appears to me that the Indian Reservations constitute a special problem, a jurisdiction within a jurisdiction. There's one other area that it seems to me many regard as untouchable, and that is the anti-diversion section with respect to the gas tax, that it must go for roads in this state. I would like to ask the members of the commission or members of the panel, "what is best?" What has been the experience in other states in trying to do away with any kind of segregated revenue?

PROF. BEBOUT: Well, I'll speak for New Jersey. We forbid segregation of revenue. We've never had constitutional segregation of revenue in the first place, under the old constitution. But we had pretty effective legislative dedication of the gas tax to roads. It was generally felt by people like the Chamber of Commerce, the League of Women Voters, the Taxpayers Association, and other groups that this was just bad business, and bad finance. So, we are maybe the only state that has an absolute constitutional prohibition against doing what most states do. And the highway lobby has been butting up against a stone wall ever since in the effort to get someone to take it seriously in its effort to get that provision out of the constitution, and replace it with a segregation provision.

PROFESSOR FARBER: I would like to respond briefly by saying that in our state it would be politically extraordinarily difficult to do away with what you might call the "dedication" feature. I'm sorry to say that over sixty percent of our revenue is in one way or another "dedicated". It's extraordinarily difficult for intelligent legislative decision-making to take place in the light of price fluctuation, escalation of costs, and the uncertainty of federal funds. It makes for feast or famine financing. It precludes rational comprehensive fiscal planning. Even a teacher's lobby that should know better, would scream bloody murder if we were to touch funds dedicated to education. This has been one of the major obstacles to a very broad gauge, very serious constitutional revision in our state. You are very fortunate if you didn't have such provisions, for once in, it is very difficult politically to become free.

40

PROFESSOR BEBOUT: I can't refrain from just adding a thought. We have one dedicated fund which I forgot. This is the so-called "school fund". It was put in there in 1844. It dedicates the interest on a few hundred thousand dollars to the public schools. We figured that that was surely obsolete because it costs more than a few thousand dollars to support the public schools in New Jersey. But that great intellectual organization, euphemistically known as the New Jersey Education Association, made it very clear that if we took that out of the Constitution they'd beat the constitution. Well, we correctly assessed the intellectual level of that outfit and left the school fund provision alone.

PROFESSOR FELLMAN: I think that if there's any point on which professional students of American government would agree it is that constitutionally segregated funds are a big nuisance, and that they deny the legislature the flexibility it needs to adjust to the problems of the state as they develop. But, the subject that you raised, Bill, brings up the broader question of rethinking the whole problem of how to create a more responsible legislature, less hampered by minute constitutional restrictions so that it can use its best judgment from year to year as the legislature confronts the problems of the state. I suppose, as I said last night, the main reason for the wordiness of our constitutions is the distrust of the state legislatures. If you go back and study the history of the United States, there were very good reasons why that distrust developed.

I hope that the commission will give great thought to what it can do to free the legislature from unnecessary constitutional shackles so that it can operate effectively, as a responsible body. This involves other things that I think we have to give thought to if we are to make our legislatures more efficient and more effective bodies. You have a wonderful example of the distrust of the legislature in your constitution. Your constitution makes it very clear that at least the constitution is based on the notion that the less the legislature is in session, the better off the people are apt to be. And so they've got these very stringent limitations on how many days you can sit per year. I should think that a properly organized legislature should be free to sit as many days as it needs to accomplish the business of the state. Now I would be opposed to any restriction on the length of the legislative session. Let the legislature decide that. But I think this argues for better legislatures than we've had in many states. For example, I think legislatures badly need staff services and legislative aids of all kinds so that they can do their work more intelligently on the basis of more information. There are many things in a legislative structure that need thinking and reorganization. I happen to think that the legislature is at the very heart of state government. In my opinion, the most important public act in the state is the adoption of the annual or biennial budget. This is the real key to what is going on in the state. Charles Beard used to say in his dramatic way to his students: "If you just show me the budget of a country, I can tell you what kind of a country it is." Just as if you know the budget of any individual, you know how he lives. If you know how a man spends his money, you can tell a lot about the kind of life he lives. And how a state spends its money is an index of how the state lives. What your priorities are is reflected in your budget. But it seems to me that all these

41

things are tied together. If you want to get rid of constitutionally segregated funds, and other restrictions upon the legislature, then you have to face the fact that we have to do a lot of work to improve the legislature so that it will be able to act efficiently and responsibly and meet the needs of the state as they develop from year to year without all the shackling of constitutional limitations.

PROFESSOR MITAU: If I may just for a moment add one thought. You, in New Jersey, were very fortunate in having only one dedicated fund. Many states have a great many of such fundamental fiscal shackles. You're going to have to experiment, for example, with newer forms of home rule and interlocal cooperation. A joint power pact, if you know what I mean by that, seems absolutely essential. The provision that the county, for example, might enter into a compact and perform common functions with other counties or local governmental units merits consideration. One-third of our 87 counties in Minnesota, some authorities contend, may no longer be viable as governmental structures. They have problems of just surviving. We need compacts, we need regions; when you're starting your search of constitutional material, be sure to provide the kind of flexibility where a state could be sub-divided into regions. We find with our people, for example, that it makes a lot more sense to speak of 11 regions in our state (one metropolitan region and ten out-state regions) than it does to speak of 87 counties.

PRESIDENT WEEKS: Senator Hirsch.

SENATOR HIRSCH: I would have liked to have responded right at the point at which an earlier speaker spoke first of all to support the conclusion that in South Dakota there is some good reason why in fact the legislature ought to be constitutionally limited. Having been a senator now for about twelve years, I can say that it's not just some wild notion that was put in the constitution. Let me say first of all that I support constitutional revision and I will always support the legislature. But let me play the part of the devil's advocate for a moment and recognize South Dakota as South Dakota is. South Dakota does not enjoy the quantity of litigation involving the constitutionality or not of a lot of the enactments of the legislature. This may be the case with a lot of other states or some other states, at least, and certainly so on the federal level. At the point when litigation occurs, South Dakota is one of the states where our Supreme Court has said and will always say that our constitution is not a grant of power, by the people; it is a circumscription of the power of the people who act through their legislature. The legislature has the power of the people to do any darned thing the constitution does not inhibit against, you might say. This gives the legislature a great deal of latitude. I think a lot of our problems in South Dakota, therefore, come about as a result of the misunderstanding of the position our own courts take with respect to our constitution. And a lot of what is generally said about constitutions does not apply in South Dakota for that reason. Let me illlustrate. I think the lawyers here who know our constitution will agree with the students of government, that for long years there must have been some time in South Dakota's history when we were carried away with the notion that

42

we could not face the coming into being any other political sub-divisions except those provided for in the constitution. In other words, the people had to grant the legislature the authority to create additional political sub-divisions beyond those which were initially provided for. We had counties, townships, and school districts. Then we had amendments and enactments that provided for irrigation districts, etc. Now, we've gotten away from that. In my time in the legislature we've had literally a host of political sub-divisions created. Whether that's good or bad is not the point. But it serves to illustrate the fact that the legislature in this state can be pretty innovative in areas where the constitution does not circumscribe its power. It is not a grant of power, as a lot of folks have interpreted the constitution. So viewed in that light, let it be firmly said that we are perhaps unique in that respect and that our problem is in large part cleaning up what we have in the current document, as opposed to putting ourselves in the position where maybe our courts could have joined with those courts that say, "Now the constitution must be a document that grants to the legislature the authority to do this, grants that the executive branch has the authority to do this, grants to the judiciary the authority to act in this area.

PRESIDENT WEEKS: Dr. Fellman.

PROF. FELLMAN: John and Ted may correct me, but so far as I know you are not at all unique, and your court is not unique in construing your constitution as one merely of limitations. As far as I know, that's the universal law all over the country. I don't know of any state Supreme Court which construes it's state constitution as a grant of power. So, I think this is a general law.

Now, while I'm on my feet, I might add, and I tried to make this point last night, that I think that it's a great mistake to think of the constitution as merely serving the purpose of judicial review. I think this is a mistake. I think a constitution has other purposes. It should not be a lawyer's document. I think it should be a people's charter. That is why I hope that when you get through with your work you can produce an interesting document, which your present constitution is not. It's unreal. You get intellectual indigestion reading that kind of a constitution. It's not made to be read, not with any enjoyment at least. And if you want the people of the state to be interested in the first principles of government, which is what a constitution should contain, then you have an obligation to state them in some interesting and readable fashion. I think it's a mistake to think of a constitution merely as a lawyer's document, the basis for litigation. Of course, our written constitutions are bodies of law. And since they are laws of superior obligation, then laws of inferior obligation must yield to them. This is the basis on which our courts practice judicial review. But I think a constitution has other purposes. I would hope that its major purpose is to educate the people into the first principles of the compact under which the state carries on its public affairs. If you approach the constitution from that point of view I think there's a certain liberating effect in getting out from under the heavy burden of thinking of it merely in terms of lawyers and judges and judicial review.

PROF. BEBOUT: I agree with everything Dr. Fellman has said. I want especially to underscore what he said about the constitution talking directly to the people. I once suggested to the drafting committee of the Alaska convention that the document ought to sing. They kept repeating that from then on. And they got a very good man who was not a lawyer as their principal consultant for the committee on drafting. He did help them to make it sing.

Now, admittedly, there must be some words of art in the constitution because it is a legal document. You have to be careful that you don't use words of common speech that get interpreted differently from the way you intended them to be interpreted in the court. I think that some confusion exists in some states over this matter of the basic nature of the constitution as a limiting, not a granting document, because of the proliferation of legislative detail in the constitution, of "thou shalt nots" directed towards the legislature, and of exceptions to the prohibitions. There are some provisions which in some states are what I call "amendment breeders". A provision in your constitution, common to most state constitutions, forbids the state or local governments to grant money or credit to any private organization. We have that provision in New Jersey, but the courts have construed it quite strictly so as to narrow its limiting effects. We are able to do most of the things that we want to do without worrying about that. In New York state, though, the similar provision has a much more restrictive effect. I think it was probably a nervous attorney general, I don't think it was the court that started this line of interpretation. Some attorney generals have done more harm to state constitutions than anybody else. Legislatures unfortunately believe attorney generals sometimes and proceed to act on their advice, and this is said without bias against a lot of friends of mine. At any rate, they said you can't give money or buy services from private welfare agencies. So we have the situation in which that provision in the New York constitution has been amended again and again, specifically to authorize the legislature to do something that it has been assumed is forbidden by the earlier provision. One of the things I would advise the constitutional convention to do is to look out for such amendment breeders. We worried about this in New York. They tried to deal with it in the late constitutional convention, but unsuccessfully, because the document was turned down.

PRESIDENT WEEKS: Is there a question back there? Yes, Representative Lacey?

REPRESENTATIVE LACEY: What about the reference to private organizations in the South Dakota Constitution?

PROF. FELLMAN: I think that the state of South Dakota is a secular state. People have a right to live here whether they are religious or not. There are many wide variations of religiosity, ranging from one hundred percent to zero among the people of the state. People have a lawful right to their views on this matter. Therefore, I would prefer that a constitution be a secular document. Now, having said that here, I would be caught dead before I raised that issue if I were a member of your commission. It just isn't worth the wear and tear. You just get the state convulsed in a great big argument about God, on Whom everybody is an expert. And so what I suggest is, and I'm sure this will be your experience, that you make some

44

practical adjustment to the facts of life. There are some things for which change exacts too high a price. But, if you ask me, if I could write a constitution to my own taste, I would make it as I think it should be—a wholly secular document.

PROFESSOR MITAU: Well, we have to be somewhat careful about speaking of the divisions of the powers of state government. All the governments of the state are divided into three distinct departments—legislative, executive, and judicial, with their duties provided by the constitution. However, when you really examine the constitution of this state or any other state, you will find this simply isn't true. In many instances, the branches are not only not distinctively divided, but the branches have to cooperate, lest government were to be seriously paralyzed. If I had the time, I could go into the executive or legislative articles to give numerous illlustrations where the joint operation of the branches of government is absolutely indispensible. And we ought to avoid making statements which simply cannot be lived up to. A practical document certainly is the fundamental charter of a great state.

I like to see a constitution which I can take into the classroom and with which I can bring about a sympathetic and constructive attitude to citizenship and government. We who talk about integrity and character would like to believe that we have a document that a critical young mind can admire and understand. It is a great moment when our young people are engaged in spiritual unity, and yet they are a part of society that is very critical.

PRESIDENT WEEKS: Yes, Dr. Farber.

PROF. FARBER: While it is not in the preamble, we do have a statement of principle. It sort of bothers me that some of the Pierre people here have not mentioned Article 6, Section 27, where it says: "The blessings of free government can only be maintained by an adherence of justice, moderation, frugality and virtue." Some of us in higher education have thought, on occasion, that the word "frugality" has been over-emphasized!

I do have one question in connection with the provision of the constitution as to the selection of the members of a convention. What would be your recommendation with respect to partisan versus nonpartisan election of convention members?

PROFESSOR MITAU: Well, very briefly, I think one of the values of a constitutional convention is that it could attract into its membership men of high standing. Moreover, you might be able to draw people into the convention that for a variety of reasons would not wish to be identified with one of the parties.

I think that, Bill, one of the first admonitions one should be aware of in reading a constitution is that it should not be read literally. The phrase that members of the convention shall be elected in the manner of the election of representatives could easily be construed to mean that there should be the same number chosen from the same sort of districts. Your constitution does not prescribe that the legislature shall be a partisan body, and I should think that any attorney general worth his salt would not find it difficult to advise the legislature on this point, that that phrase does not mean that a non-partisan constitution convention is ruled out of bounds by the language of the constitution. It just wouldn't be a very hard job to write an advisory opinion which construes that clause to mean a non-partisan convention. And if you have a convention, I hope that it would be non-partisan.

REPRESENTATIVE LACEY: Going back to the division of powers. Just exactly what is wrong with them? Now if we consider the body of administrative law, I think that we can all agree that it is in a highly fluid condition, even now. With the possible development and in the interplay of our legislative acts and judicial acts in the United States of America, they both observe the other's prerogative. So, are we assailing the doctrine of checks and balances when we assail the doctrine of division of powers?

PROFESSOR FELLMAN: May I respond to that? The Chancellor was objecting to the word "distinct." Your constitution makes a pledge that's just simply impossible to fulfill. He doesn't object to the separation of powers, he objects to the illusion that you have a "distinct" separation of powers. Actually, in modern times the chief executive of a state government or the chief executive of the United States government is primarily a legislative, and not an executive, leader. The President's reputation in history is not made by the extent to which he keeps his desk clean. His reputation depends on the success of his legislative programs. Congress cannot provide leadership itself. If it doesn't come from the White House, Congress is without leadership. It's a rather curious fact that the main business of the presidency is not executive, but legislative. It's also a curious fact that the main business of Congress is not legislative. The main business of Congress is to keep an eye on those who govern the country; that is, those in the executive and administrative branch of the government. Congress spends far more time keeping an eye on those who do govern the country, because Congress can't govern, it can only watch those who do, and see that it's properly done. That's why the investigative function of congressional committees is crucial, because this is one check (another is the annual review of the budget) by which the legislative branch keeps an eye on those who govern. It is my opinion that the greatest single weakness of the state legislature and of state government is that so many legislators are content merely to legislate. Where they really fall down is in their capacity, in their equipment, in their ability to keep an eye on those who do govern the state. In my opinion, a properly organized legislature doing a job for the people of South Dakota would spend far more time and far more energy in keeping an eye on, and supervising, those who do govern the state than they spend in passing new laws. In 30-day or 45-day sessions, about all you can do is rush a few laws through and then go home when your money runs out. It seems to me that as you revise your constitution you will have to free yourselves from this high school notion about the separation of powers, that you have an executive, and a legislative, and a judicial, and that they have nothing to do with each other. The real crunch in government arises in the interplay between the legislature and the executive and the administrative branch. The legislature cannot govern the state. It doesn't collect taxes, it doesn't arrest people, it doesn't try people. The business of the legislature is to see that those who do govern the state do it properly, efficiently, and economically.

While I'm on my feet, I want to suggest that you should not take out of the constitution the beautiful statement about frugality and virtue which Bill Farber mentioned. It's a lovely statement, it's been there a long time, it expresses a noble ideal, and I'm afraid that if you should take it out, people will accuse you of being against frugality and virtue, and then you're sunk.

MR. TREMERE: Professor Fellman has talked about how the constitution ideally would be a people's document. Professor Bebout talked about the difficulties that states have had with lobbies, and so on. My question is directed toward anyone. Is it the function of the Commission to sell the idea of revision or the revised constitution to the public? And if it is, how do they go about it?

PROFESSOR BEBOUT: I said this morning that either a convention or a commission has the responsibility of presenting the suggested changes to the people or in the case of the commission, directly to the legislature. There is an obligation to explain and in effect to advocate the changes that they propose. If they are not worthy of their advocacy then they ought not to be presented. It seems to me just as simple as that. What the commission can do beyond that, collectively and individually, will depend partly upon its license from the legislature. Conceivably, the legislature might give the money to conduct a state-wide "educational" campaign. I use the word "educational" in quotes. You know, you can educate for a purpose. This would be fine. The New Jersey convention and other conventions have done this with the resources that the state made available to them.

Let me add further, that I don't think that you're going to get any substantial improvement of your constitution, whether by the commission route or by the convention route or a combination of the two, unless a new constitution develops a citizens' concern. One reason why the Maryland constitution went down to defeat was that the convention had the foolish idea that the lower they played this, the better. Maybe it could be true in a low vote. I had an argument with the president of the convention on this question on the last day of the convention. I said, "You may think that everybody's going to lie quiet, but I predict that they'll come out of the wood work just two or three weeks before the election. The people are going to be confused and they'll do the natural thing and vote 'No'." I don't often say I told you so, but this is exactly what happened. Now he admits that (he said so publicly in Philadelphia the other day) what they should have done was have a strong, affirmative, citizen's campaign. The convention could have helped, but it should have been financed and run mostly by independent citizen groups. We never in this world would have gotten the revision in the New Jersey Constitution (one of the most conservative states in the Union), if it hadn't been for the fact that there was a citizen's committee for constitutional revision on the job continuously from 1941 to 1947 which spent upwards of a million dollars. This was back some years ago when a million dollars was worth more than it is now. There is just no point in getting into this business unless you're ready to make a large commitment.

I do want to make one comment, though on this business of political energy. Some political energy may, when it's expended, be gone, used up.

Sometimes the center of political energy is like the center of energy in a reactor. It generates energy. We feel that this is what happened in New Jersey. We spent a terrific amount of political energy over nearly a decade to get a new constitution. But that increased the political muscle of the citizenry of the state. Governor Driscoll led the legislature and the citizenry immediately following the adoption of the constitution in a complete review of local government in the state and the adoption of what I modestly claim to be the best optional municipal charter law on the statute books in any state. This would not have happened if it had not been for the continuing effect of the energy generated by the constitutional revision effort.

PROFESSOR MITAU: I'd like to add something to this comment if I may. I think that your commission would have to decide quite early what scope their activities are to encompass. It seems to me that through the device of public hearings subsequent to your organizational and preliminary programs, you can conduct an educational campaign.

PRESIDENT WEEKS: Thank you. This session of the Dillon program stands adjourned.

IV. Saturday Afternoon:
G. Theodore Mitau

DEAN ADAMS: The last man on the program has a very tough spot. Everything has been said, it seems, and everybody is anxious to go. For that reason, the selection by the committee of who would be last was a very difficult thing to do. I think we've done wisely. The first two speakers have done excellent jobs. Chancellor Mitau will now close this with his speech which I'm sure will make this one of the best Dillon Lectures we've had. Chancellor Mitau.

Partial Constitutional Revision Through Piecemeal
And Comprehensive Amendments:
Reform Patterns Of The 1960's

G. Theodore Mitau
Chancellor
Minnesota State College System
(formerly of Macalester College)

Among professional students of state government, and particularly among the group represented at this conference, there is little disagreement as to what generally distinguishes a good constitutional model from that of an unsatisfactory one. We would all agree, I suspect, that constitutions should be "brief and to the point"; that they should facilitate intergovernmental relation and cooperation; that they should avoid unnecessary detail duplication and restrictions; that they should permit the linking of political power with responsibility so that "those who have power can be held accountable and those who are held accountable may then in turn have the power commensurate with their responsibilities"; that unlike statutory codes, state constitutions should concentrate on fundamental principles; that they should provide a framework within which legislatures, executives, and the public can strive to adjust or adapt governmental structures orderly and periodically in this era of enormous social, technological, and cultural change.

Whatever the precise nature of structure and language, modern American state constitutions must permit much more effective problem solving in

49

governmental and political settings characterized by population shifts and urban growth, by demands for expanded public services and individual rights, by requirements of political leadership and professional expertise, and by electorates who seek a more authoritative role in the making of decisions that effect "their lives, their fortunes, and their sacred honor."

Thus, when the past legislative session in its wisdom created a constitutional revision commission "to provide for and enter into a comprehensive study of the Constitution of the State of South Dakota to determine ways and means to improve and simplify the constitution," it offered to the people of this state a unique opportunity to move towards substantial improvements in the quality and efficiency of its government. While it is rarely prudent or propitious for a visitor to catalog the shortcomings of his host, there are, of course, situations where professional criticisms may in fact be invited and welcomed. What makes a possibly indelicate task so much easier for us today is the availability of analytical background material by some of your own scholars and commissions whose studies already provide ample and persuasive evidence for the need of constitutional revision in this state.

Without endeavoring to particularize each of the following, any brief compilation of some of the major criticisms of this state's constitution would probably have to include the following:

1. Various constitutional provisions are excessively detailed, obscure, dispersed, or obsolete.
2. The state's executive branch is diffused among a relatively large number of elective officials, boards, and commissions. The terms of office in many instances are too short, and the governor's power to name appointments is inadequate.
3. Regular legislative sessions are constitutionally restricted to 45 days in odd-numbered years and to 30 days in even-numbered years— a questionable limitation on legislative power.
4. The judiciary is administratively over-decentralized, and the elective judicial terms are quite short.
5. State and local government is weakened by long ballots for non-policy making positions, by constitutionally imposed fiscal restrictions, by unrealistically low debt limitation, and by insufficient provisions for the consolidation of governmental functions performed by counties, municipalities, and special districts.
6. Constitutional provisions are lacking for a legislative post audit, for the joint election of the governor and lieutenant governor, for systematic executive reorganization, for the periodic submission to the electorate of the question whether a constitutional convention should be called or for a formal vote by the electorate on a newly framed constitution, for more explicit safeguards of an accused in criminal trials or before legislative or administrative tribunals, for the prevention of racial discrimination, and for the greater protection and management of natural resources.

No one acquainted with contemporary realities of American state and local government will see anything very surprising in this summary indictment of South Dakota's Constitution. Whether or not misery loves company, it is a widely acknowledged fact that these types of constitutional infirmities are found in the overwhelming majority of the states and that they represent major factors that helped to impede the forward movement of American federalism.

What is often forgotten is that nearly eighty percent of our state constitutions were written in the eighteenth and nineteenth centuries, that they addressed themselves to predominantly rural and thinly populated communities, and that they reflected a political philosophy deeply suspicious and fearful of government in general, and of executive power in particular. "Unlike the ten commandments in brevity, directness, or authorship," American state constitutions "were framed with the explicit purpose of further restricting the power of the elected officials—elected particularly, after the Jacksonian era, for short terms and for clearly limited duties."

Hemmed in by highly detailed and restrictive constitutions written for a very different America, our state and local governments found themselves totally unprepared for the demands of the twentieth century. Industrialization and urbanization, world war conditions and economic crises, population explosion and revolutionary changes in transportation and communication—these as well as other more recent developments combined to constitute challenges that greatly exceeded the fiscal and governmental resources available at the state level. Frustrated and newly activated electorates increasingly turned to Washington for services and programs that governments nearer to them were either unable or unwilling to provide.

Were this trend to continue unabatedly, little, indeed, would be left of the federal model. Fortunately for those who still attribute significant value to a revitalized state and local political system—and this includes diverse forces and spokesmen across the ideological spectrum—powerful voices and influential power groups throughout the nation have begun to battle for constitutional and governmental reforms which might yet bring the states into a more effective partnership with the federal government. Hopefully it may not prove too late to assist in the self-renewal of our fifty laboratories in self-government.

South Dakota's charter of 1889 with its 73 amendments and over 30,000 words could be formally revised by at least two fundamentally different processes: the calling of an unrestricted constitutional convention or by piecemeal amendment. The staging of such a convention has already been discussed. There are a great many advantages in viewing and working on the needed constitutional changes in a systematic and comprehensive setting. Most political scientists consider such conventions "to be the most efficacious method of conducting thorough-going constitutional reform." Related subject matter may be properly integrated and inconsistencies eliminated. A carefully prepared, professionally staffed, and properly representative constitutional convention provides an excellent arena in which to debate and resolve basic considerations of policy substance.

Numerous legal and political obstacles abound, of course, to the successful convening of such an assembly as well as to the subsequent ratification of its work by the voters. Legislatures must give their assent to the calling of the convention; in this state a two-thirds majority is required. Such proposals have been defeated here twice, once in 1914 and again in 1924. The whole process of completing constitutional revision through the convention mechanism consumes a great deal of time; a minimum of five years are required in South Dakota as in most other states. Assuming initial success at the legislature, the voters must then pass on the question of the call; the next legislative session must enact the operational and statutory details for the convening of the convention, its staffing, and for the election of the convention's membership. At the ensuing general election follows the election of convention members, and three months later the delegates would convene to begin their months of deliberation. Then, unless a special election is called, the new document would have to receive majority approval at an upcoming general election.

That such a complex and prolonged procedure offers great opportunities for opponents of change to marshal their forces and obstruct the course towards reform must be obvious. Legislators may be apprehensive that a convention might upset district lines and the distribution of legislative power. Conservative interests may fear the expense of the venture, the possibility that radicals would dominate the proceedings, or that untried governmental experiments would find their way into the basic charter. Taxpayer groups might resist new revenues or socialistic efforts at redistributing the wealth. Local government officials might oppose the consolidation of counties, municipalities, or special districts while state officials might be most antagonistic to administrative reorganization and to strengthened gubernatorial control. Fear of the unknown, such as those pertaining to the composition of the convention or the effect of substantive changes, tends to heighten the political suspicions and antagonisms between organized labor and employers' associations, between urban and rural voters, between conservatives and liberals.

In the light of these realities, constitutional revision *via* piecemeal amendment, while certainly no panacea, does offer some relative advantages. Those who favor this method emphasize its possibilities for speedier and less expensive change, a generally more-than-even chance for voter approval, and a greater legislative inclination to go along. Among the chief weaknesses in this approach are the tendencies towards fragmented and often inconsequential changes or the attainment of a superficial sense of reform in the absence of truly substantial accomplishments.

As is often the case in American politics, the day-to-day pragmatic adjustments that are brought into play to meet the pressures for institutional changes are so great that the debates of the academicians tend to be overshadowed by the events themselves. A survey of the actual constitutional reform efforts of the last decade reveals some additional options that seem to lie somewhere between the traditional convention and piecemeal approaches. For want of a better term, I suggest we call them partial constitutional revision through comprehensive amendments. Before elaborating this concept further it might be more appropriate to block out in broad relief an overview of some of the major events in state constitutional developments during the past decade.

    1. There is considerable evidence to support the contention that both the volume and the pace of adopting peacemeal amendments has increased notably during the past decade, evidence which in Professor Bebout's words "clearly reflect the accelerating obsolescence of many parts of state constitutions." Whereas fifty to fifty-

five percent passage rates were common in the past, the 1968 elections produced results indicating that nearly seventy percent of the proposals submitted met with voter approval.

2. Major constitutional revisions were achieved through the device of adopting comprehensive amendments in Florida (1968), Wisconsin (1967), Iowa (1968), Massachusetts (1966), California (1966), and Pennsylvania (1968), but failed in Idaho (1966).

3. Limited constitutional conventions were authorized in New Jersey (1966), Tennessee (1968), Pennsylvania (1967), and Connecticut (1965).

4. Entirely new constitutions were accepted in Michigan (1963) and Hawaii (1968), but rejected in Kentucky (1966), Rhode Island (1967), New York (1967), and Maryland (1968); Calls for constitutional conventions were approved in New Mexico (1969), Arkansas (1969) and Illinois (1968); Voters in Vermont turned down a proposal for a convention in 1969.

Upon closer examination, the record of reform obtained through partial constitutional revisions becomes even more impressive. Even the briefest analysis of a few of the 448 piecemeal amendments added in 1966 and 1968 indicates something about the nature of governmental changes. Among the major state actions were these:

Alabama—Constitutional officers were authorized to succeed themselves.

Arizona—Executive officers were given 4-year terms and legislative salaries were increased.

Colorado—Executive departments were to be limited to a maximum of twenty and provision was made for a joint ballot for governor and lieutenant governor.

Idaho—Allowed annual sessions, gubernatorial appointments for court vacancies, and procedures for the removal of judges.

Kansas—Adopted annual 60-day legislative session.

Louisiana—Governor was allowed to succeed himself (prior provision permitted only one term.)

Mississippi—Permitted consolidation of courts.

Montana—Provided for continuity of state and local government in emergencies.

Nebraska—Authorized an income tax.

Nevada—Permitted county consolidation and authorized increases in judicial pay.

New Mexico—Abolished justices of the peace and established magistrate courts.

North Carolina—Authorized legislative pay raises.

North Dakota—Authorized municipal home rule.

Tennessee—Reduced residence requirements for voting in presidential elections and authorized consolidation of local government functions.

Utah—Approved annual legislative sessions and increased compensation for legislators.

Washington—Authorized increase in state salaries during term of office (excepting the legislature).

West Virginia—Provided for an executive budget.

53

Wisconsin—Provided for a single ballot for governor and lieutenant governor, four terms for executive constitutional officers, and for legislative determination of judicial salaries.

Much more important, of course, for quality improvements in constitutions was the impact of various comprehensive amendments successfully ratified in a number of states, especially those in Massachusetts, Pennsylvania and California.

For example, when the voters of California in November of 1966 approved proposition 1A by nearly 3-to-1 margins, they accomplished with this one amendment alone some very substantial constitutional revisions. As Professor Hyink reports in his recent essay, the changes affected almost one-third of the constitution.[1] Obsolete language was eliminated, inconsistent provisions stricken, and the much reduced wording became more precise. Legislative power was enhanced by providing for unlimited and unencumbered annual sessions in place of the previous required alternating between limited regular and budgetary sessions. Legislative salaries are now to be fixed by statute although increases may not exceed five percent per year and the raises must be approved by a two-thirds vote in each house.

In the new article on the executive, provisions were made to define the line of succession by statute, to clarify the process of determining a gubernatorial vacancy or disability, to remove salaries from the basic charter, and to permit the governor "to assign and reorganize" executive functions.

With respect to the judiciary, the comprehensive amendments strengthened the District Courts of Appeals (in the hope of easing the excessive workload of the Supreme Court), stiffened the eligibility qualifications for judges of all but the municipal courts, and prohibited judges from seeking appointive or elective posts during their terms of office.

At the same general election at which Californians voted for these constitutional changes, the people of Massachusetts too were willing to support some major alterations in their 1780 document. In Professor Bebout's view, the four general amendments "added up to more extensive constitutional revision than has resulted from limited conventions in some states or from efforts of constitutional revision commissions in some others." As a consequence of these additions, voters in Massachusetts can now vote for governor and lieutenant governor on a joint ticket, the chief executive is authorized to reorganize the administrative departments "if not acted upon by General Court within 60 days," state and local authorities may assist industrial developments, and home rule is extended to municipalities on a "residual power basis."

If comprehensive amendments seemed to be traveling the high road in California and Massachusetts, they proved even more successful in Pennsylvania. At a primary election in May, 1967, the voters approved eight amendments including provisions which stipulated that:

(1) The legislature be a continuing body for two years and empowered it to call itself into special session;

(2) The governor and lieutenant governor be elected jointly;

---

1. "California Revises Its Constitution," *The Western Political Quarterly,* XXII (1969), pp. 637-654.

(3) Electronic voting devices be permitted in the legislature; and

(4) There be an accelerated method of amending the state constitution in time of emergency (approval of two-thirds of the members of each house of the legislature publicizing the full text in newspapers throughout the state; approval of the voters in a statewide election at least one month after passage by the general assembly).

Also approved was the call for a limited convention "to modernize" the rest of the constitution by February 29, 1968. After this instructed group finished its task and submitted its numerous proposals in the form of five major amendments, Pennsylvanians once again registered strong approval and passed all five of them on April 23, 1968. Fundamental revisions were incorporated into the articles dealing with the judiciary, local government, legislative apportionment, state finance, and state taxation. Among other provisions, there was established a single, statewide court system with centralized administration; nearly all judges and justices must now be attorneys; a judicial inquiry and review board was created composed of judges, lawyers and laymen; all units of local government, including counties, were declared eligible for home rule charters and for intergovernmental and area-wide powers; debt limits were to be legislatively determined (except that Philadelphia's debts were not to exceed 13.5 percent of the assessed valuation of its taxable real estate); provision was made for a five-man apportionment commission and for state Supreme Court action if this group should fail to act; and restrictions on the state debt and fiscal operations were greatly eased.

Whatever shortcomings attach to partial constitutional revision, and despite occasional setbacks as in Idaho (1966) and in California (1968), the record of the comprehensive amendment process now seems sufficiently impressive to deserve wide professional attention. While it is accurate to say that political circumstances, behavior patterns and cultures vary from state to state and between the diverse regions of the nation, it may still be true that competent students who have analyzed the campaigns in California and Pennsylvania should be able to offer us some insights into the reasons for success or failure that could prove instructive and relevant in other jurisdictions.

In order to give such amendments the best possible chance for acceptance it appears a number of essential conditions and requirements should be met—prescriptions, to be sure, applicable in varying degrees to other forms of constitutional revision as well. First, great care should be exercised in obtaining adequate assistance from professional staffs and consultants for the preparation of the necessary background studies, reports and supportive evidence. Second, broad organizational support should be built across political party lines, economic interest groups, and socio-ethnic alignments. Third, specialized groups with staff and membership primarily dedicated to enlisting public approval for the amendments should be established and work on a full-time basis. Fourth, publicity efforts should include maximum endorsement by the various news media, disseminating stickers, signs, pamphlets, fact sheets, special releases and other forms of campaign literature and devices. Fifth, leading political and civic figures should be asked to lend their active support to articulate the expected benefits from the proposed constitutional revisions. All in all, optimum efforts would have to be generated to persuade generally apathetic publics that "everybody who is anybody" favored the changes, that a modern constitution would provide more efficient and competent governmental services, and that the state capitol, city hall, and court house would have to be unshackled if the trend to centralized government in Washington is to be reversed and local citizen involvement and participation given greater meaning and power.

Unless such efforts are expanded and political coalitions effected, narrow visioned interests find it relatively easy to arouse voter apprehension. Proposed constitutional changes will be alleged to entail dangerous or radical deviations from established governmental traditions and practices, to permit shifts of power from local electorates to arbitrary bureaucracies, or to raise taxes since restrictions would be removed and public spenders given free reign. While our science of politics has as yet not matured to the point of formulating precise laws of political behavior, it may be suggested on the basis of accumulated experience that the intensity of political opposition would tend to be somewhat greater the wider the scope of the revision effort. With unrestricted conventions leading in terms of breadth of scope, and single amendments occupying the opposite end of the revision continuum, the method of comprehensive amendment or that of the single amendment would seem to be more suitable to states with conservative electorates and interests. If Professor Clem's analysis of South Dakota politics is correct, we find this to be a jurisdiction where power is diffused, party organization weak, the governorship powerless, the legislature restricted, and politics candidate-oriented rather than issue-centered.[2] In such a political and constitutional climate, resort to the comprehensive or single amendment process might prove more practical and rewarding. At that, when it is recalled that the adoption rate of single amendments in South Dakota stays close to the fifty percent mark (1948-1957, 51.4 percent; 1958-1968, 51 percent) which is below the national average, it becomes quite clear that massive effort will have to be launched before any meaningful constitutional revision can become feasible.

The responsibility for preparing this state for constitutional change now rests first and foremost with the 13-member South Dakota Constitutional Revision Commission and its secretariat, the state's Legislative Research Council. This Constitutional Revision Commission can accomplish a great deal if it is willing to work hard and conscientiously towards its goal. Much ground has already been broken by similar commissions now operating throughout the country. Various studies by their research staffs and publications issued by the Committee for Economic Development, the National Municipal League, and other groups will prove helpful. In the final analysis you will have to fall back on your own professional resources as you address yourself to your particular situation and needs. Some years ago when I conducted a study of Minnesota's constitutional development, I concluded that the people of the state owed "their constitutional commission a profound debt of gratitude for the care with which it phrased its recommendations, for its professional and scholarly approach, and for its

---

2. See generally Alan L. Clem, *Prairie State Politics: Popular Democracy in South Dakota,* Washington: Public Affairs Press, 1967.

lively concern for the possible and practical. Entire sentences in subsequent amendments (to our state's 102-year-old constitution) could be traced back to the language of the Minnesota Constitutional Commission Report; the amendments themselves often served as substantive implementation of the commission's prescriptions." Hopefully, some future commentator tracing the accomplishment of your group will arrive at a similar judgment concerning the results of its efforts.

But now let me end on a caveat. Much of the research done in the realms of state governmental reorganization and constitutional reform is still dominated by lawyers and legal technicians. How much hard evidence have we in fact accumulated to prove that the strong governorship and the hierarchical arrangements of bureaus, longer legislative sessions, and a more integrated judiciary will in fact by themselves produce a better quality of government. Many of us believe that it will, but much of our conventional wisdom is in need of much more critical scrutiny and better scientific foundation. Let us enlist our colleagues in the social sciences to help us examine these widely held hypotheses by the most rigorous and analytically sound tests. Many of the policy questions and problems posed by constitutional reform are neither abstract or esoteric. They call for pragmatic solutions within a democratic model which is severely challenged from within and without. Those of us who treasure the art of self-government must constantly rededicate ourselves to provide our political processes with the best possible framework of law. As scholars and as citizens we should be certain that our state constitutions facilitate and encourage public policies which would afford all of our people the possibility for maximum self-realization through individual or collective efforts and which would help to create the formal institutional arrangements through which all of us could work to improve the quality of government and the quality of life.

DEAN ADAMS: It is time for comments; which of you gentlemen wants to be first with the last? Well, how about you, Dr. Fellman?

PROFESSOR FELLMAN: I think that was a very fine statement by Ted Mitau on the problems which are involved in a piecemeal constitutional revision; and I think I made it clear this morning that that is my preference if the choice is between that and a convention. And I suspect that is reflected in the nature of the resolution, or the bill, adopted by the legislature creating this commission. I don't want to sound like a common scold, if I restate a point that Chancellor Mitau has just made, merely for emphasis. I would think that among all the factors which are involved, if the work of this commission is to be successful, I should put at the very head of the list the obligation of members of the commission to take this assignment seriously, and to work at it. It is not an easy assignment; it is a very demanding one. I do not wish to be misunderstood when I say that all of us in this room have much to learn, and those who are responsible for such a serious matter as revising a constitution—which after all, is a going thing in this state—have a great deal of information to acquire and understanding to be deepened before they venture to suggest changes in the basic charter of this state to the voters. It will require a great deal of reading. There is a large and complex literature on the structure of state constitutions. There is a large literature on all of the special problems of state government, on the selection and tenure of judges, on the office of the governor, on the structure and functions of the legislature, and so forth. This is not an easy assignment. I know, since I served on such a commission for many years, that it is possible to slough along, but that merely means that someone else will do the work for you, and do the thinking for you. If this is to be taken seriously, this is not a simple assignment, and it is not one which will be fulfilled very easily.

I thought I might contribute to this discussion without repeating what Chancellor Mitau has said if I made brief reference to my own experience with constitutional revision in Wisconsin, a state not terribly unlike yours, although we have many more people, and we have a great metropolitan center on the lakeshore. About ten years ago when the present, and very able junior senator, Gaylord Nelson, was elected Governor, he appointed on his own responsibility a governor's commission on constitutional revision, and he put me on that commission. It was a commission of fifteen.

As I look back I think one of our weaknesses was that the legislature was insufficiently represented in the commission. The governor put only two legislators on the commission, as I recall. I think that was a mistake. Many members of the legislature were very suspicious of the commission, and regarded us as a bunch of the governor's "busy-bodies". It would have been wiser to have a stronger representation from the legislature. In this sense I think your commission is well constituted. You have very good bridges between this effort and the work of the legislative body. Furthermore, we were a non-statutory body. We had no statutory existence at all, and therefore no appropriation at all. We didn't even get reimbursed for travel. The people who came into Madison for meetings came at their own expense, and put themselves up at the hotels at their own expense. The only public expense involved was the printing of the final report. The governor and his assistant looked around and they found some money someplace and we got it printed. That was the only public expenditure. Well, we had a curious and unhappy political situation. We had a Democratic governor and a Republican legislature. Nothing happened when we published our final report after about two years of work. We drifted along without any change occurring as the result of our efforts. Governor Nelson served two two-year terms, and then went to the U. S. Senate. John Reynolds, another Democrat, was elected to succeed him. Since we had made no progress with constitutional revision, he reappointed our commission, again without a statute, and without an appropriation. He included most of the people who had been on before, he took some off who had not done much work, and put on some new people. We worked for another two-year period. Towards the end of that period, many of us were full of despair. We'd worked hard and we had made some very sensible proposals. We were rather depressed at the almost complete lack of response from the legislature.

Now, one of the last things we did was have a great big rousing argument over the question as to whether we were on the right track or not, that perhaps we should go for a convention. And finally, on the last day of our last meeting, by a vote of 9 to 8, or 8 to 7, I've forgotten which, a very narrow vote anyway, we finally endorsed the convention as the proper way to get constitutional revision. The legislature paid absolutely no attention. The rest of the story I can tell very quickly because if you were listening to Chancellor Mitau, you heard the results. In the last four or five years almost every suggestion we made has been written into the constitution.

The lesson I learned was that you don't need a convention. That if you come up with the right ideas, if you are right in the positions that you take, eventually you will find a hearing. Eventually the legislature will respond and the voters will respond. We have modernized our constitution in a remarkable degree by this process of piecemeal revision. I can't help but moralize, since I'm a moralist at heart, that those of you who are engaged in this process of constitutional revision would be well advised to take your time—to take all the time that you need. The state is not going to collapse if you take a little time to study this matter thoroughly, and to be very patient once you've made your final report before you see the fruits of your labor. But if you labor properly and with due diligence and make sensible and intelligent decisions, I think that you will eventually modernize and revise your constitution.

DEAN ADAMS: Thank you Professor Fellman. Now Professor Bebout, it's your turn.

PROFESSOR BEBOUT: Somewhat earlier today Professor Fellman tried very hard and conscientiously to start an argument. I'm afraid that I'm not going to be any more successful, if as successful, as he in breaking the harmony of thought that we have displayed, but I am going to make a slight effort. First, I want to say that I think Professor Mitau's statement was a masterful piece. I'm looking forward to adding it to my archives. I agree with him and Professor Fellman mainly in that I don't really have a preference between revision by a commission followed by legislative amendment, and a convention. I don't think it's possible to have a general preference for one or the other. I think that there are certain circumstances in which one method is indicated, and other circumstances in which the other method is indicated, and some circumstances in which a combination of methods is needed. As I said before, I think the commission phase was absolutely essential to the modernization movement in New Jersey. I think the ultimate convention was in that state also essential. As a matter of fact, there was (I may have mentioned this before) an interim point when the legislature followed the advice of the commission and submitted the question to the people whether or not the legislature could be authorized to act like a convention and submit the proposed new constitution to the people. People voted overwhelmingly "yes" on that question, and the 1944 legislature acted as a bicameral constitution convention, reviewed the work of the commission of 1941 and 1942 and submitted a document very similar to the one that the commission proposed. The people turned it down enthusiastically. They turned it down partly because of the political atmosphere in the legislature in the doing of this job. Then, three years later they overwhelmingly approved almost the same constitution when it came from the convention. Nobody in 1940 when Governor Edison "foolishly" (because he didn't know anything about state government or anything about the constitution) made the calling of the constitutional convention his principle campaign plan. Nobody would have guessed at that time what sequence of events would ultimately produce a new constitution. It's a very good thing that Governor Edison didn't know more about practical politics, because if he had, he never would have been so foolish as to talk about constitutional revision in 1940.

I do want to say one other good thing about conventions. Professor Fellman raised some doubts about the quality of conventions. Well, conventions are human beings in a particular context, just like legislatures and university boards of regents and any other groups of people. They have all the strengths and weaknesses of people. I've observed a good many conventions, that is, considering the number of them, and it is my judgment, and this is a subjective judgment, that on the average, they stacked up probably a little better than legislatures in terms of the level of education, general sophistication, and public dedication. This is a reasonable expectation because a convention is a one-shot proposition and it attracts, generally speaking, people who feel they can't afford for one reason or another to go into politics to the extent necessary to be in the legislature. When it does attract legislators, it attracts, generally speaking, legislators with somewhat more than average understanding and concern for fundamentals. Now this isn't always true. New York was plagued by too many legislators who just acted the way they do in the session in Albany along about May of every year. Incidentally, we used to say in New York that while we didn't have constitutional limitations on the length of the sessions, we had a practical one. It was the closing of the racing season in Havana (laughter). We don't have a racing season to go to in Havana anymore, but they still end up about the same way and in the same kind of log jam (laughter). I'm just going to say one more thing. It seems to me that what we've heard today indicates that the inventiveness of the American system has not run out. We've had constitutional conventions ever since before the Revolution. We've had constitutional commissions off and on for more than a century and a half. But the last period, since World War II, and especially the last ten years, has seen new developments, new facets brought out in both of those old institutions and new potentials in the combination of them. A political society, if it is going to survive, has got to maintain this creative, innovative capacity. One of the reasons why at least four days a week I am more of an optimist than a pessimist about the American future is that it seems to me that the spring of creativity is running just as strongly in our system as ever.

DEAN ADAMS: We certainly appreciate the contributions each of you have made. I'm sure the close attention by the number of people evidences that. Now, the real credit of the success, I believe, of this particular series goes to Dr. Farber. It was his idea, he arranged the presence of each of these experts. I think we owe him a hand—and also for the meal last night, which was very good.

PROFESSOR FARBER: I think that this has been a wonderful occasion. It has been a very fine way to get the Constitutional Revision Commission started on its obviously onerous but challenging and worthwhile task. I think that we should be appreciative of the scholarly and stimulating work that has been done by our speakers.

I thank you all for the excellent attendance at these sessions. I would like to bring these sessions to a close with a challenging and provocative quotation from De Toqueville's *Democracy in America.*

I am tempted to believe that what we call necessary institutions are often no more than institutions to which we have become accustomed, and that in the matters of social constitutions that the field of possibilities is much more extensive than men living in their various societies are ready to imagine.

Appendix A. Data on 50 State Constitutions
Index Scores (see notes for derivation)

State	Number of Constitutions[1]	Length[2]	Number of Amendments Adopted[3]	Constitutional Change Index[4]
Georgia	5	5	5	15
Louisiana	5	5	5	15
Alabama	4	5	5	14
South Carolina	4	4	5	13
California	2	5	5	12
Florida	4	4	4	12
New York	4	4	4	12
Texas	4	4	4	12
Maryland	3	4	4	11
Virginia	4	4	3	11
Arkansas	4	4	2	10
Delaware	3	3	3	9
Nebraska	2	3	4	9
Pennsylvania	3	3	3	9
Colorado	1	4	3	8
Massachusetts	1	4	3	8
Mississippi	3	3	2	8
Missouri	3	4	1	8
North Dakota	1	4	3	8
Ohio	2	3	3	8
Oklahoma	1	4	3	8
Oregon	1	3	4	8
South Dakota	1	4	3	8
Idaho	1	3	3	7
Illinois	3	3	1	7
Kentucky	3	3	1	7
Michigan	3	3	1	7
Minnesota	1	3	3	7
New Mexico	1	3	3	7
West Virginia	2	3	2	7
North Carolina	2	2	n.d.	?
Maine	1	2	4	7
Indiana	2	2	2	6
Iowa	2	2	2	6
Montana	1	3	2	6
New Jersey	3	2	1	6
Rhode Island	1	3	2	6
Tennessee	3	2	1	6
Utah	1	3	2	6
Vermont	3	1	2	6
Washington	1	3	2	6
Wisconsin	1	2	3	6
Wyoming	1	3	2	6
Arizona	1	2	2	5
Connecticut	1	1	3	5
Kansas	1	2	2	5
Nevada	1	2	2	5
New Hampshire	2	1	2	5
Alaska	1	2	1	4
Hawaii	1	2	1	4

Source: **The Book of the States, 1968-69,** Chicago: Council of State Governments, 1968, p. 15. Data adapted for this table by Alan Clem, who is also responsible for the definitions of categories and the CCI in the notes below.

1. 1 = one constitution. 2 = 2 constitutions. 3 = 3 or 4 constitutions. 4 = 5 or 6 constitutions. 5 = 7 or more constitutions.

2. 1 = less than 10,000 words. 2 = from 10,000 to 19,999 words. 3 =

63

from 20,000 to 29,999 words. 4 = from 30,000 to 69,999 words. 5 = 70,000 or more words.

3. 1 = fewer than 20 amendments. 2 = from 20 to 59 amendments. 3 = from 60 to 99 amendments. 4 = from 100 to 199 amendments. 5 = 200 or more amendments.

4. The Constitutional Change Index is the sum of the three scores for the state. Note that Civil War-related state constitutions increased the CCI for most southern states, and that comparatively recent statehood decreased the CCI for most western states. An alternative derivation of CCI might be based solely on length and number of amendments adopted.

Appendix B. Members of the South Dakota Constitutional Revision Commission

Representative Charles E. Clay of Hot Springs
Professor William O. Farber of Vermillion
Judge Jon Fosheim of Huron
Representative Woodrow K. Hawley of Brandt
Professor John F. Hendrickson of Brookings
Senator Robert Hirsch of Yankton
Senator Arthur L. Jones of Rapid City
Senator Richard F. Kneip of Salem
Representative Charles Lacey of Sioux Falls
Mr. Wallace McCullen of Rapid City
Mr. Laurence M. Stavig of Sioux Falls
General Neil Van Sickle of Rapid City
Professor I. D. Weeks of Vermillion

Appendix C.   A List of Participants
(in order of appearance)

Donald E. Habbe, Dean of the College of Arts and Sciences and Professor of Government, USD.

David Fellman, Vilas Professor of Political Science, University of Wisconsin.

John E. Bebout, Professor of Political Science, University of Texas at Arlington, formerly Director of the Urban Studies Center and University Professor of Political Science at Rutgers, the State University.

G. Theodore Mitau, Chancellor of the Minnesota State College System and Professor of Political Science, Macalester College.

William O. Farber, Professor of Government, Chairman of Department, and Director, Governmental Research Bureau, USD; member, South Dakota Constitutional Revision Commission.

Thomas C. Geary, Professor of Government, USD.

I. D. Weeks, Professor of Education and former President, USD; member, South Dakota Constitutional Revision Commission.

Neil Van Sickle, Major General, United States Air Force, (retired); chairman, South Dakota Constitutional Revision Commission.

Bernard Linn, Commissioner of School and Public Lands, State of South Dakota.

Charles Lacey, South Dakota Representative; member, South Dakota Constitutional Revision Commission.

Jon Fosheim, Judge, Ninth Judicial Circuit of South Dakota; member, South Dakota Constitutional Revision Commission.

Alan L. Clem, Professor of Government and Associate Director, Governmental Research Bureau, USD.

Robert Hirsch, former South Dakota State Senator; member, South Dakota Constitutional Revision Commission.

Blair Tremere, graduate student, Department of Government, USD.

James R. Adams, Dean of the School of Law, USD.